Achieving Excellence in Management

"A unique approach among management books with much wisdom and useful advice. A valuable companion text for a graduate student or a seasoned executive."

Dr. Rod McColl
Professor of Marketing
Rennes International School of Business, France

"Little is known about bad management which can be more important than the numerous success stories often difficult to emulate. This book considers both in a constructive manner and helps us perform better in the future by understanding the past."

Leo Paul, Dana, BA, MBA, PhD
Researcher, Author, and Journal Editor
University of Canterbury, New Zealand

"A very informative book with interesting case examples. Especially useful for those of us who have specialised in subjects other than management."

Larry Eaker
Academic Director
Masters Program
Essec Business School, Paris

"This unique approach of focusing on bad management and its negative aspects makes a stronger case for good management. Some of the many good examples could perhaps benefit from more detail. Extensions to international, SMEs and various crises gives a current relevance to the book."

W. Alan Randolph, PhD
Director Center for Global Business Studies
Professor of Leadership and International Business
Merrick School of Business, University of Baltimore

"A concise, very readable text elaborating many useful techniques with concrete examples. Anyone who aspires to achieve excellence in management should keep this book handy."

J. Ronald Collins, PhD
Professor and Director of International Programs (Retired)
School of Business Administration
University of Prince Edward Island, Canada

"With its contrasts of bad versus good, the book is an important contribution to the literature on general management. Its many interesting and relevant examples will be most useful to those already having some business experience."

David Gillingham, PhD
Academic Director
Kaplan Higher Education Institute

"The book uses an effective 'hands-on' approach and is a pleasure to read. It is full of useful applications and new ideas. The management performance aspect, so important today, could perhaps be further developed."

Dr. J.-M. Heitz,
Professor and Director of Studies
La Rochelle Business School, France

Achieving Excellence in Management

Identifying and Learning From Bad Practices

Andrew Kilner

First published in 2010 by
Business Expert Press, LLC
222 East 46th Street, New York, NY 10017
www.businessexpertpress.com

ISBN-13: 978-1-60649-122-5 (paperback)
ISBN-10: 1-60649-122-9 (paperback)

ISBN-13: 978-1-60649-124-9 (e-book)
ISBN-10: 1-60649-123-7 (e-book)

DOI 10.4128/9781606491225

A publication in the Business Expert Press Strategic Management collection

Collection ISSN 2150-9611 (print)
Collection ISSN 2150-9646 (electronic)

Cover design by Jonathan Pennell
Interior design by Scribe, Inc.

First edition: February 2010

10 9 8 7 6 5 4 3 2 1

Printed in Taiwan R.O.C.

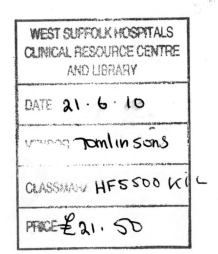

This book is a weapon in the fight against bad management and is dedicated to all those who have suffered from its effects.

Abstract

Most books on management principles focus on particular rules of thumb and best management practices. While the latter approach provides useful guidance and insights, it does not give executives much of an understanding of what bad management can entail and the damage that it can produce. Indeed, good management makes the most sense when it can be directly contrasted with examples of bad management and its implications.

To fill this critical gap, this book adopts a fresh approach, identifying cases of bad management from real-life business situations experienced by the author (chapter 3) and contrasting them with good management practice as concisely defined in chapter 2.

The sound management principles so developed can subsequently be applied to a broad range of settings for personal careers in traditional enterprises or adapted to management of small firms (chapter 5) or international companies (chapter 6). Also, they can be used to establish role models and mentor topics for individuals (i.e., ideal managers) and excellent companies (chapter 4).

The last chapters show how good management practice can be applied to better handle a wide range of current world problems faced not only by companies (chapter 7) but also by national governments and international institutions (chapters 8 and 9) during these particularly uncertain times.

Finally in the appendices, there are two specific cases illustrating the usage of rigorous management techniques to analyze events and situations outside the company business arena.

This book will be of interest to practicing managers and to students of management. It can be a useful support to mainstream academic books for current students but is of greatest value to postgraduates in their first or second job, for older managers who have not previously been exposed to this kind of material, and for various researchers or counselors who could further develop certain of the novel themes proposed here.

Keywords

Good Management, bad management, management excellence, management errors, management failings, practice, processes, skills, roles, managers, ideal managers, respected managers, small firms, international companies, world crises, political systems

Contents

Figures

CHAPTER 1

Introduction

Why Is There So Much Bad Management?

The initial problem is that lots of people in business still don't know what management is, and, of course, this makes it impossible to go further and understand what *good* management is.

The worst culprits are those who try to convince you that management is just common sense and "do it yourself" abilities that they claim to possess partly from intuition and partly from their past experience. If this were so, then the world of teaching and research could be largely regarded as a waste of time. Most, however, will probably say that management is a combination of topics such as marketing, finance, logistics, and so on, whereas in fact these are only (departmental) management *functions*.

The real basis of management are the four management *processes* of planning, organizing, leading, and controlling, which are used in all departments like marketing planning or financial control.

Allied to these are the management *skills* necessary to carry out these processes, of which the three main categories are technical skills, interpersonal skills, and conceptual skills.

Even today most managers have not studied these topics seriously, partly because courses in management processes, fairly common in North America, are rather rare in Europe. Their "substitutes" under such names as organizational behavior (OB), or "politique generale," do not uniformly cover the whole required field. So as well as having past experience, and a suitable character, managers need to have learned how to use the various skills and how to apply the relevant processes. This will be further developed in chapters 2 and 3.

How Did You Choose This "Good Versus Bad" Approach?

The initial impulse came the day a student at the bachelor level told me that my lecture examples of good management were obvious: "Of course a good manager should be an effective communicator, make the right decisions, and so forth," he said. I then realized that I had learned much more from having been around bad managers than from good ones; with the latter, things went along smoothly just like a plane on autopilot. However, it would be wrong to focus too much on bad management. What is needed is to identify examples of bad management that one should avoid and to contrast them with the good management that one should learn to practice.

What Does This Book Do?

This book does the following:

- Succinctly clarifies the practice of good management based on a rigorous application of management processes and related skills (chapter 2)
- Identifies numerous examples of bad management practice using real-life situations that I have personally encountered (chapter 3)
- Assesses the characteristics of "ideal" managers and "excellent" companies to serve as models for others to follow (chapter 4)
- Applies the good management practice to various situations where managers might be working: small, local firms (chapter 5) and those operating internationally (chapter 6)
- Analyzes responses to economic crises since the year 2000 and discusses how the current key management issues can be handled by companies, governments, and others (chapter 7)
- Elaborates management methods that could be applied to several other areas of activity like problems in the international environment and political systems (chapter 8)
- Reviews management practices of the recent past and likely future and suggests what aspects will remain and what will need to change (chapter 9)

How Does It Compare With Existing Books?

Firstly, there are books written by academics principally for business school students that are very comprehensive but too "heavy" to handle for self-tuition on a daily basis. Secondly, there are books written by consultants, some of which tend to be rather too simplistic, for instance, suggesting that you only need 10 steps or 24 hours to master management. Some serve to introduce various fads implying that by simply using these fads, one can sort out one's problems. At the top of this academic or consultant pyramid are certain business gurus who have become world famous through their books and by running exciting conferences with rather simplistic recipes. In some cases their personal experience of management can be very limited—one recently indicated that he had had only two experiences, with two different bosses. Thirdly, there are books written by famous managers who have demonstrated a record of high performance in the business world. The problem here is that their recipes for success are rather haphazard and of course relate to their own achievements in the situations with which they were faced. Many of these methods cannot be applied by other managers in different situations who have different personalities and skills from this author's.

These limitations also became apparent when I was selecting part-time lecturers to teach in our management department. Many of the academic candidates suffered from having too little industrial experience. The company managers gave interesting examples of cases from within their companies, but these were rather haphazard and not always closely related to the theoretical course material that the students had been given in previous lectures. Certain consultants were better at combining theory with practice, but that practice was essentially based on what had happened to others rather than to themselves.

So What Are the Special Features of This Book?

This book tries to combine the pertinent elements from my varied background as a company manager, an academic, and a consultant, as well as my experience of starting up and running my own firm, albeit only on a modest scale.

Apart from the innovative approach of contrasting the bad from the good, it adopts a systematic, rigorous treatment taking management practice to new levels of usefulness, not only in conventional business, but also in their application to other areas of activity. As well as analysis of much private research not available elsewhere, it includes many histories from real life that occurred to me personally or that I witnessed firsthand. It is rather concise and makes for easy reading on a plane as well a good reference to use in the office. At every stage it tries to add value by giving the reader indications as to how he or she can improve his or her own management understanding and performance.

What Is Its Target Audience?

The main targets are graduate students in their first or second job and older managers who have not previously been exposed to these topics. Current business school students will also find it a useful support to their basic academic books. Finally, workers in other fields like politicians, advisors, journalists, and researchers may appreciate the management approach and novel suggestions and ideas presented in the last three chapters.

PART I

Good and Bad Management

CHAPTER 2

Essential Fundamentals

It is first necessary to remind ourselves of the basic management tools that managers use, in other words, *skills* and *processes*. These will also serve as a framework for the subsequent discussion regarding the managers' performance, be it good or bad.

But, even prior to skills and processes, we must consider resources and environment, as these are pretty much imposed on managers and independent of the abilities that the individual may possess. This is particularly important in this kind of study since clearly a manager's performance could depend to a large extent on the type of environment in which he has to function and the quantity and quality of resources that he has available at his disposal.

The Business Environment

Any systematic study of management should start by considering the environment in which the firm operates. It is unfortunate that this is not done in many business school programs, where the environment may be examined later if it is examined at all.

The business environment can be depicted as a series of concentric rings around the firm. The outer ring consists of the *external macroenvironment* and includes such environments as the economic, the political, the technological, the legal, and so on.

The next ring inward is the *external microenvironment* in which we find these other organizations that work closely with the firm, for example, its customers, suppliers, bankers, and so on.

Separately, we also need to consider the particularities of the environment in the *industry sector* in which the firm is operating. Among the key factors here are those of industry complexity(C) and industry stability (S), either high or low. Each of the four types possible under these two headings (high C–high S, high C–low S, low C–high S, and low C–low S; Figure 2.1) will involve different methods of operation and hence require different types of management.

Degree of
Instability

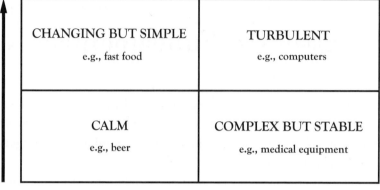

Figure 2.1. Types of environments.

Resources

In the very inside ring, that is, in the actual firm, are the available resources that the manager has at his disposal. These include the physical facilities, equipment, finance, workers and staff, and the information and knowledge possessed by the firm.

Clearly it is easier for a manager to manage if he has more and better resources at his disposal, but many tend to dissipate these resources and eventually perform no better than their "poorer" competitors.

Management Skills

Management skills fall under a number of distinct categories. As well as noting elements in each category, it is useful to mention where the skills could have been obtained.

The first category is *personal skills*, which includes such things as intellect, energy, honesty, empathy, and so on. As the name implies, these skills are inherent in the individual person's character: many since youth, others acquired at a later age like adaptability (mobility combined with flexibility), which is one of the key attributes for graduate employment.

The second group of skills is *technical skills*, some of which are learned and some of which are developed. Learned skills include such abilities as languages and computer knowledge but also less standard ones like time management. Developed skills arise from professional experience starting off with company internships and consist of things like turning action into results, selling new ideas, and so on. A deeper knowledge of one function (e.g., purchasing) and at least one business sector (e.g., automobile) should be obtained to enhance one's personal marketability.

The third group of skills is *interpersonal skills*—that is, those dealing with people. These include activities such as communicating, motivating, staff selecting, and coaching. Communication has many facets, and there are means of assessing and improving each one: *written* (e.g., by preparing a one-page executive summary of a report), *oral* (e.g., by an effective presentation in front of a group—for which participation in a debating society is excellent training), and the least-known, *listening* (understanding what has been said before speaking). We learn from listening rather than talking, and yet, during so many discussions (e.g., TV panels), several people talk at the same time and do not listen to the others.

The fourth group of skills, *conceptual skills*, relate more toward the task and consist of such skills as analysis, problem solving, decision making, innovation, and others acquired later in life like vision and judgment.

To these four categories it is useful to add a final element, like the spices in a newly cooked dish. Thus, we include exemplary behavior and the ambition and will to win not only for oneself (as many selfish managers do) but also for one's team and indeed the whole organization. These skills can be summarized in the following list (with full details given schematically in Figure 2.2):

- Personal qualities
- Technical skills for effective operational performance
- Interpersonal skills for handling a team or department
- Conceptual skills for strategic development of the organization
- Integrating skills that weld together the whole group

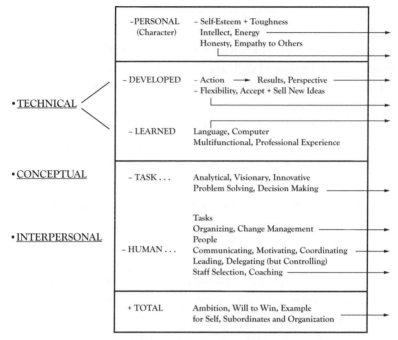

Figure 2.2. Qualities and skills of an ideal manager.

Roles

Before moving on to the next section, it is useful to mention the various roles that individuals in the firm need to fill.

The *management roles*, as defined many years ago by Professor Henry Mintzberg, are 10 in number, split into three categories as follows:

- *Interpersonal*: figurehead, leader, liaison
- *Informational*: monitor, disseminator, spokesperson
- *Decisional*: entrepreneur, disturbance handler, resource allocator, negotiator

Most managers will only perform a few roles, but company leaders, especially those who have launched their own firms, will have to fill most of them themselves, which is quite a formidable task! (Today, due to the wide current usage of computers, the role of disseminator is now outdated.)

Team roles, often known as *Belbin roles*, relate to the different roles of members of a team brought together to accomplish a specific project. They include roles such as those of coordinator, monitor, implementer, and plant (ideas person). It is important for everyone who is likely to work in a project team to have identified the roles for which he or she is most (and least) competent so that the team leader can rapidly constitute his team with a suitable person for each role.

Management Processes

As already mentioned, these are the real heart of management and will be summarized as follows.

Planning

Planning is the conversion of a chosen mission into specific actions according to this sequence: missions, goals, strategies, plans, and actions. The following are different types of plans:

- Continuous plans (every year for 3 to 5 years)
- Strategic plans (periodic)
- One-off plans (e.g., launching a major event, small firm start-up)
- Plans for new projects (why, where, who)

Continuous plans have normally been made as a projection on what has happened in the past. *Strategic plans* are based on the concept of "back from the future" that is starting from the question "Where do we want to be?" They are done periodically, especially at the time of big changes like mergers.

One-off plans for launching events are a very good way of training in management processes. The author has used this widely as a student project in his course whereby, working in groups, the students organize a major event such as a school gala or an expedition to a remote part of the world. The elements deal with each of the five management processes, and each student in the team is responsible for writing one element of the total package.

A *small firm start-up plan* is a classical example of one-off planning.

In his courses on small business management, the author supervised the preparation of more than 500 such plans of which around 30 have been real projects that were actually launched. As depicted in Figure 2.3, the business plan consists of an executive summary followed by appropriate sections for each function (marketing, operations, etc.), with the financial details being calculated at the end. The writing of each section is the responsibility of one individual student for which he gets a specific mark to add to the overall grade for the whole group project. Students are told of the paramount importance of a good executive summary for all reports—particularly in the business plan, without which high-level

---

SMALL BUSINESS START-UP PLAN CONTENTS

EXECUTIVE SUMMARY: One- or two-page overview of key items

COMPANY DESCRIPTION includes background, current status

PRODUCT OR SERVICE OFFERED with its unique features and choice of location

MARKETING PLAN following Market Research Process

OPERATING PLAN including Distribution/Logistics

MANAGEMENT: Roles/competencies/experience

LEGAL FORMAT with reasons for choice

AID & ASSISTANCE available from different sources

FINANCIAL PLAN: Funds required, future projections (including tax issues)

APPENDICES of drawings, tables of data, etc.

Figure 2.3. Small business start-up plan contents.

reviewers or investors will never read it. The ability to convey the essence of the venture within a 10-minute presentation is also essential.

New project plans, such as that for the development of a new product, require a somewhat different approach. These projects are normally handled by a multifunctional team who needs to answer a number of key questions at the outset of the project. These questions are summarized in the outline shown in Figure 2.4.

In all aspects of planning there is, of course, a time element. In continuous plans, this exists naturally on an annual or even monthly basis.

WHAT is to be done?	Objectives, specifications
WHY does it need to be done?	Importance, priorities, conflicts
WHERE is it going to be done?	Place of delivery, sourcing
WHEN is it required?	Start/completion dates, intermediate control points
HOW is it to be achieved?	Sequential tasks, procedures, resources
WHO is involved?	Who is in charge and has individual responsibilities

Final Assessment Criteria	
COST	Within allocated budget?
TIME	Within planned time frame?
QUALITY	Within required specifications?

Figure 2.4. Project and action planning sheet.

For the others, a timetable must be carefully prepared with the completion and launch dates being very important criteria.

As a final comment, one has to acknowledge that there has always been a resistance to planning and this has greatly increased during recent years as the environment has become more volatile—and violently so since 2008. However, even without considering the accuracy of the figures, the planning process is useful in itself. What is certainly necessary today is when preparing the plan, to consider more possible options and the risks that a changing environment may provoke. When, hopefully, the environment will again become more stable, the companies that take planning seriously will show superior performance, like the Emerson Corporation that, placing great importance on planning, achieved 40 years of unbroken profit growth.

Allied topics within the planning process are *problem solving* (PS) and *decision making* (DM), which are often considered together because PS is typically followed by DM—that is, to make the decision to execute the agreed-upon solution. Some factors to consider in PS are identification of the exact nature of the problem, the sequence or methods of evaluation, using individuals or groups, and the novelty or urgency of the matter. Some factors for DM include the following: aim for a consensus after a free discussion, delay verdict if that helps and if it is not urgent, and act quickly after a decision is made. Note that, if problem solving abilities are valuable, then it is even more desirable to anticipate problems before they occur.

Organizing

Organizational Structure

The organization's total workload is divided into tasks that are then allocated to specific groups or departments. Certain departments need to be centralized, while others are devolved to operate in a more independent fashion. This process needs to be done in a coherent manner and cannot just follow the fashion of the times that may favor one or the other.

Organizational structuring requires evaluation of the relative importance of control, rapid customer service, availability of staff, and operating costs and can thus vary from a simple centralized functional organization to an organization with units devolved by place, product, customer, a hybrid of these varieties—or a system using a matrix format involving function and product for example.

Organizational Style

Organizational style varies from bureaucratic or mechanistic hierarchy at one extreme to organic and flat at the other. It depends partly on environment (complexity and stability) and the age or size of the firm; also, for *manufacturing*, it depends on the technology process (continuous or batch) and for *services*, it depends on whether the service is routine, like cashing checks, or nonroutine, like consulting a lawyer. (Note that bureaucratic can still be the most effective form today for certain sectors like hotels, parcel delivery, etc.)

Organizational change involves a transformation of structure and style. It is normally prepared by considering both "hard" issues like reengineering and "soft" issues like empowerment and resistance. This subject has now become so important that it is often taught as a course (often called "Change Management") in its own right rather than as part of management processes.

Staffing

(This additional management process is usefully included here, although its elements are similar to those of the human resource management function.)

Once the nature and position of departments has been decided under organizing, it is necessary to staff them with appropriate people. The sequential steps in this process are as follows:

- *Before*: job definition, search, interviewing, selection and hiring
- *During*: training, evaluating, promoting
- *After*: parting, future staff planning

Without going into great detail on standard procedures, the key elements of selection and hiring are twofold: A person is hired not only on competence alone, as many rejected candidates should realize, but also on the fit of the new person into the organization—particularly toward his boss and his fellow workers.

Once hired (often at significant cost), new staff members will expect suitable training and a salary progression or eventual promotion based on realistic and fair evaluations. If these processes are not carried out effectively, the best people will leave, the mediocre who cannot readily find alternative employment will stay, and the overall performance level and reputation of the organization declines. What is worse, some of those wishing to leave will get themselves made redundant and obtain severance payments at a further cost to the organization.

Future planning for managers departing or retiring takes place only in the very best organizations. The Emerson example is again worth quoting: Potential successors to the remarkable Chuck Knight were evaluated over a period of almost 2 years and eventually, not only was the best one selected, but also his highly competent rival was persuaded to stay in an almost equally high post!

Leading or Directing

The leading process does not only concern heads of big organizations but also everyone who has been charged to supervise a group of people in a department or similar unit.

Unless such leaders can use strong sanctions (when their staff will obey through fear), the leader has to adopt a certain behavior to impose his authority. This is commonly an alternance between friendly and tough exhortations (e.g., the carrot and the stick) or by taking up a suitable position between the extremes of authoritarian and democratic behavior. The exact position chosen depends on the characteristics of the leader (e.g., natural authority), on the nature of the followers (willing or unwilling), and on the situation (e.g., routine or crisis). The leader's natural, personal orientation (e.g., more people oriented or more task oriented) will also be a major factor in the success or failure of his efforts.

Motivation is one key element in the leader's armory in getting his staff to achieve the desired objectives. There are numerous ways of motivating people and genuine respect is the simplest (and least costly). It is amazing what can be achieved by just telling someone, "Thank you, that was a job well done."

Communication, the other key element, should flow easily both up to the boss and down to the staff with it being informal rather than formal as much as possible. External communication will obviously depend on whom it is directed (e.g., customers, shareholders, etc.) but needs to be realistic and honest if future credibility is not to be impaired.

Delegation of selected tasks to appropriate people, if done correctly, will be gladly accepted, as will *management development* programs to help suitably chosen staff acquire new skills such as coaching and dealing with conflict. These practices will produce multiple benefits in motivating existing staff, in ensuring future management availability, and in reducing the leader's workload to enable him or her to concentrate on the important tasks of vision, strategy, and change.

The *manager versus leader* distinctions are not clear-cut: each has to perform some roles that may be thought of belonging to the other (see Figure 2.5 for examples of leaders using management processes). However, broadly speaking, leaders are responsible for effectiveness, namely, that the organization reaches its goals; this will often mean initiating appropriate change. Managers are there to handle complexity and ensure the efficiency of carrying out existing operations. The four-box chart of complexity and instability related to the industry environment can again be used to illustrate these points (Figure 2.6).

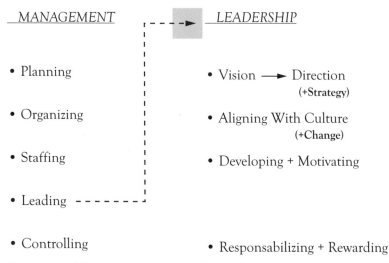

MANAGEMENT   LEADERSHIP

- Planning

- Organizing

- Staffing

- Leading

- Controlling

- Vision ⟶ Direction
  (+Strategy)

- Aligning With Culture
  (+Change)

- Developing + Motivating

- Responsabilizing + Rewarding

Figure 2.5. Management aspects of leadership.

Degree of
Instability   <u>and need for Leadership</u>

Figure 2.6. Needs for managers or leaders.

Controlling

Control is the reverse side of planning; it ensures that plans are met so that the organization moves to achieve its goals, the first part of the plan of course being the budget of the current year. For *internal control* within the firm, the main control instruments are the *four financial statements*:

- Profit and loss
- Balance sheet
- Cash flow
- Break even

For ease of quick understanding, these can be compared to the instruments in a car to measure progress of a journey to a specific destination (goal) as shown in Figure 2.7.

In parallel, we also measure the following:

- *Financial ratios*: assessing liquidity, leverage, profitability, risk
- *Individual operational activities*: level of stocks, capacity utilization

> ### Financial Control Instruments
> ### The Car Journey Analogy

Input Requirements:

- CAR & FUEL   - FACILITIES & RESOURCES

- DRIVER & PASSENGERS   - MANAGER & STAFF

- DESTINATION & ROUTE   - GOALS & PLAN

Measures of Progress:

- SPEED OF TRAVEL   - PROFIT & LOSS STATEMENT
  (Speedometer)   (P & L)

- DISTANCE COVERED   - BALANCE SHEET
  (Milometer)   (B.S.)

- FUEL SITUATION   - CASH FLOW STATEMENT
  (Gas Gauge)   (C.F.S.)

- REQUIRED AVERAGE SPEED   - BREAK-EVEN POINT
  (Trip Computer)   (B.E.P.)

Figure 2.7. Financial control instruments: The car journey analogy.

One should note the close relationships between the three control approaches as they are assessing the key elements of profit, cash, debt, and break even, thus, for instance, stocks converted to cash, capacity utilization affecting break even, and leverage affecting debt on the balance sheet.

Control of other parameters has been referred to in previous sections:

- *Projects* (under planning): within time-frame, budget, and quality norms
- *People* (under staffing): performance evaluation

Because of many failings in recent years, it has been thought appropriate to add a further control aspect to this list, namely, *external control*, which encompasses various bodies that should act independently of the firm, such as auditors, nonexecutive directors, supervisory administrators, accreditation agencies, regulators, and so on. Examples of their actions will be discussed in chapter 3.

Conclusions

This chapter thus provides a concise summary of the essential tools of good management. The key "processes" portion has also been summarized in the form of a "ready reference" chart at the end of the book (Figure 10.1).

CHAPTER 3

Management Failings

Having laid down a systematic framework and indicated some elements of best practice, it is now time to analyze a wide range of examples where managers are continually making mistakes.

Planning

Continuous 5-year planning was a hallmark of the larger multinational firms. It was largely based on projecting forward past and current trends, so that, if things were going really well, the projections tended to become completely unrealistic. I recall working in the synthetic fiber industry where, if our projections had continued, the usage of the natural fibers wool and cotton would have largely disappeared by now! Another amazing projection came from the Sinclair Company, inventors of the first digital watch and the ZX 81 personal computer. The sales had such a rapid take off that, if carried forward at the same rate, would have had Sinclair becoming larger than IBM within 5 years!

Besides excessive optimism, one of the main culprits is unqualified forecasting, which is not stating the key assumptions (such as oil prices and inflation rates) that underpin the forecast. The same kind of thing applies to future surveys in all types of activity. Thus, in the sporting arena, if asked who will win, we could reply, "Our team X has a good chance, but only if they continue to play at the level they did in their last game."

Strategic plans came into wider usage later but the concept of "working back from the future," in other words, from where we actually want to be, is still not generally practiced. Of course, the danger here is similar to the projections discussed earlier, namely, that people's ambitions may be too unrealistic.

The need for well-prepared one-off plans is now largely accepted, especially when it comes to business plans for a new start-up. However, the current trend to encourage young people with no business studies toward creating their own business frequently leads to problems. Without training in preparing a convincing business plan, they are unable to secure private investment. They are thus forced to approach local support agencies for funds for their projects—mostly restaurants or boutique type stores, which are not only risky but also do not contribute much to the economy in terms of employment, exports, or growth prospects.

Planning new projects, if one follows the why, where, who outline previously mentioned in Figure 2.4, should lead to a successful outcome. However, to take this further, I would also propose a rigorous evaluation of the "3Rs," which can save much fruitless discussion or getting unwisely involved in many off-the-cuff suggested ventures. The 3Rs consist of the following:

- *Realism* regarding relationship to strategy, achievability, and risk
- *Resource* availability (or how obtainable)
- *Return* in terms of debt as well as sales and profit

Problem Solving

The first essential is to identify the problem and decide whether it is sufficiently important to spend time on resolving it or whether it is better to go around it and do something else. Then it is necessary to constitute a group or team who will study the problem and come up with alternative solutions.

In practice, study groups tend not to provide enough alternate solutions, subjectively favoring one solution over others rather too early and stressing all its advantages while minimizing its disadvantages. Also, they often don't identify the possible constraints and consequences on the organization in terms of cost and other factors. While they can make a recommendation as to the best solution, the final decision needs to be made by a strictly objective decision-making committee.

Another frequent error is the confusion between a rather urgent short-term requirement and more elaborate long-term solutions. I recall the information technology department telling us what wonderful things they were developing for the future while we were facing daily operational problems that had to be solved quickly. Another fairly similar case in outside business life was the serious traffic problem at a traffic circle in our locality. Based on my previous experience in transportation, I came up with a possible short-term solution that could be implemented in a week at negligible cost. I received a long reply from the mayor detailing the studies that were now taking place and the possible wonderful solution that would arrive—possibly in 2 years time!

Decision Making

The decision-making process must ensure that the best solutions to problems or the best suggested opportunities are selected and put into practice. To arrive at "the best" will usually require a free discussion of the proposed alternatives and a maximum concensus among the participants if they are to put their heart into its implementation. Thus, autocratic leaders who restrict such discussion risk ending up with wrongly chosen or poorly executed projects.

During a meeting to decide MBA pricing, a rather authoritarian dean imposed his own view based on his (exaggerated) perception of the nature of the program and reputation of his school. Prices were raised toward the levels existing in the best schools and, not surprisingly, his eventual intake of students was drastically reduced compared to original expectations.

Another common source of error is the speed with which the decision is made. It is now considered a sign of weakness not to make decisions rapidly, and, as it is even worse to go back on a decision, many bad decisions are made and can continue to cause difficulty for a considerable time. One can observe this regularly among politicians and football referees. On the contrary, it is better to take some time over a decision, especially if it is an important one, as long as, of course, it is not very urgent. However, one has to take care not to fall into the habit of avoiding making decisions because they are too difficult or because not enough time has been allocated for the decision-making process. Leaders with an extremely democratic orientation often tend to fall into this trap, which I have frequently witnessed.

There is nowadays a reflection as to how far people should be sanctioned for making bad decisions. The variation in standards on this matter among different occupations is really immense. A Wimbledon tennis referee was once replaced after confirming two bad line calls, and a musician in a top orchestra may suffer a similar fate with two false notes during an important concert. In stark contrast, many businessmen, and particularly politicians, seem to survive having made bad decisions of far greater importance.

Organizational Change

Change management has been one of the most common practices during recent years. As with many such activities, however, it has often been abused, particularly by the less competent managers who, starting new into an organization, wanted to be seen doing something different. Of course, the need for change was essential in many situations. "Hard" change in restructuring to reduce the number of operating units and make the company more competitive is one example. Equally, "soft" change was useful for companies that had just been privatized or deregulated.

In order to be more responsive to local customers, organizational structure tended to move more toward devolved units, and in order to empower people and speed up decision making, organizational culture moved away from hierarchy and toward a flat "organic" configuration. However, it was often forgotten that all change had a cost, not only in creating the new structures, but also because operations were invariably upset during the changeover process. Substantial financial charges thus had to be taken on the balance sheet during such a process.

The other extreme to frequent change is of course to resist any change at all. Like many conscientious employees, I would often come up with suggestions to improve certain things. But there were always some managers who would tell me that these things were working reasonably well already, so there was no reason to change them. Some of these people just did not want to be bothered with the effort that this change would involve, whereas others were completely unaware that these things were *not* working well!

Staffing

As previously mentioned, the topics under staffing are similar to the activities practiced by the human resource department. Unfortunately, many organizations do not place a great value on this department; one of the most alarming statements that I ever heard was the director of a business school saying that, just because the school taught human resource management, it did not mean that he had to pay undue attention to it in his own organization!

The selecting and hiring of staff is, in my opinion, one of the major reasons for the existence of bad management. It was suggested in the previous chapter that the two key aspects of good managers were competence and being able to fit into the team in which the new person would be working. However, even if both factors seem to be present, there is no guarantee of success. Thus, there was a case where director A fired two people whom he himself had originally hired a year or two previously.

An even worse example was that of director B, a new managing director appointed from the outside into a family-founded firm where I was working. He judged that the existing directors were rather old-fashioned and should be removed or sent into retirement. (He only kept the finance director as he realized his value and importance to his own ends.) New candidates that he chose replaced the other five directors, but unfortunately three of the five proved to be unsatisfactory and were subsequently replaced.

How is it possible, one may ask, that such incompetent directors were themselves appointed to their position? It is clearly not feasible to find out the real reasons, but the feeling was that director A was moved out of headquarters and "sent out to pasture" in the subsidiary prior to retirement, and director B was a very good friend of the chairman of the parent company. There are obviously many other such possible reasons, and it would be interesting to research the topic further.

Moving on to performance evaluation, this is an activity that should serve both to develop the employee and to improve his contribution to the work of the company. However, in many companies, the procedure is treated simply as an administrative task, often based on a very badly designed evaluation document. In other companies, it is used as a means to put pressure on the employee to work harder, or as a prelude to a possible removal from the firm if he does not perform better in the future.

For those involved in the performance evaluation procedures, I should like to suggest a system that served me well in the past. This is based on having a meaningful discussion with the employee and avoiding conflict that can poison the whole atmosphere from the start. It begins by complimenting him on the things that he did well and then asking whether there were other things where he felt that he did not do so well. It is the employee himself who therefore brings out the weak elements of his performance, and you can then support him by discussing what can be done to improve his work in this area in the future. The meeting thus ends on a friendly note with a remotivated employee rather than a bitter one.

The removal of staff by firing, redundancy, or other methods is surely the most unpleasant part within the working environment of today. It is a vast field of study, and I will restrict myself simply to a few situations that took place in firms where I was working.

The first situation concerns threats made to a staff member who dared to criticize activities in the firm even with the genuine objective of improvement. "If there are so many things wrong here, you are always free to leave" would be a typical reply, even to a worker who was making an important contribution to the firm. This worker's input and appropriate skills would be badly missed on departure and during the time it took for a new replacement to be found (if one could be found). The second situation involves the firm's obligation to the fired employee; when firing people, the firm has to give them the statutory salary payment in lieu of notice. The same departing employee often only received this money on condition that he signed a statement to refrain from making any comments on what had really happened either to other members of staff or certainly not to anyone outside the organization.

Leading or Directing

The techniques previously suggested in chapter 2 can be applied to many diverse situations. Let's take the example of the carrot and the stick procedure in lecturing to rather undisciplined students in an academic institution. In my own case, because of my position, age, and experience, I managed to have sufficient natural authority, so I would not need to threaten to use the stick very often (figuratively, of course, as usage of a real stick is no longer allowed as it was in my youth).

However, for many new lecturers, often looking no older than the students whom they are teaching, the situation can be very difficult. I recall the case of a young lady law lecturer who went to the "stick" extreme and got very angry and upset. This conflict developed more and more to an extent where the students began to call her all kinds of rude names. Despite condemnation of the students for their behavior, there was no alternative but to change the lecturer.

At the other extreme, we had a "carrot-type" lecturer who gave in to all the student's wishes regarding topics discussed in the lecture. The students continually made him go off on a tangent with the net result that at finishing time, he had only covered half the required material.

The best leaders rarely have to go as far as to rely on sanctions, and aspiring candidates can train themselves in this regard. An extraordinary example was the rather quiet girl elected president of our first MBA student class. She had no sanctions at her disposal but, with much effort, succeeded in getting the group to accomplish several extracurricular projects that they had been unwilling to get involved in. This experience served her well in the future when, appointed as director of studies of the undergraduate program, she had to handle a wide range of difficult situations with dissatisfied students and their parents.

The carrot and the stick is a simplistic example of the spectrum between the extremes of democratic and autocratic leadership. As previously mentioned, many leaders have a character at either end of these extremes and do not realize that it is necessary to modify it according to the situation and the nature of the people they are leading.

In a business school with which I was familiar, there was a director at the autocratic end of the spectrum. He was quite efficient, but people did not dare to contradict the views that he would put forward, some of which were obviously not optimal. When he departed, his successor was quite the opposite—a very democratic person who allowed everyone to give his or her input. The problem, however, was that this took up a lot of time and, at the end of the meeting, the agenda was not covered nor the required decisions made.

Another key spectrum concerns the interest in people as opposed to the interest in tasks. The ideal manager should be interested in both, but most of us tend to favor one more than the other. I recall working with two lecturers who are good examples of each kind. The first was a man from Scotland teaching human resource management, always willing to have a chat with you or with the students, even using student-type colloquial expressions. However, one had to be careful in asking him to do a detailed project as this was not one of his strengths.

The second was an English woman who had a doctorate in engineering and taught operations management. She was more reserved and less sociable, but her lecture notes and any task she did was perfectly done.

A similar spectrum to these examples exists for people paying great attention to detail as opposed to those who only want to see the broad picture. While working for a UK company as a business research and development manager, I was put under a director who was extremely fastidious; every report that I wrote had to be rigorously analyzed and had to contain no spelling mistakes. Very few of the things that we proposed were actually taken forward. When this director was moved elsewhere, I had a new boss who was the exact opposite: he was almost too keen to try out new suggestions, and I often had to restrain him by saying that the project really needed more analysis. Having to handle such a drastic change in the character of one's boss was not easy at the time, although now one can regard it as a valuable experience. This same story includes another very related spectrum: the spectrum between reflection and execution. Usually the "detail" people prefer a longer period of reflection, and the "broad" people prefer more rapid implementation. Again, a point of balance needs to be found for each specific situation.

It is tempting, if not strictly accurate, to try to combine these features to create two distinct leader personality types: one who is human oriented, broad, flexible, and informal and the other who is task oriented, detail minded, more rigid, and more formal. It would also probably emerge that, on average, the first type tends to be more democratic and the second more autocratic.

Motivation and Respect

Motivation of staff is one of the main functions of leaders. There are, of course, many diverse methods of motivating people that partly depend on the type of staff and the particular situation. I recall the comments of a French graduate who went to work in England for a company where people are provided with company cars (the higher their rank, the better the car), which they can proudly exhibit on the driveway of their house. This did not motivate him in the least, he said; what he would have preferred was a higher salary and longer vacations.

However, there is no variability with regards to people wanting to be appreciated and respected. It is one of the great puzzles of the business world that, despite massive evidence from research and from surveys indicating that respected staff members perform better, so many bosses still do not heed this advice. How can this be?

In my view, there could be one or more possible reasons. Firstly, some leaders want to emphasize their position above that of their staff, and showing too much respect or friendliness may undermine their status or make it more difficult for them to make unpopular decisions or to resist staff claims for bigger rewards. This is truer of leaders in continental south European countries as opposed to more egalitarian Scandinavians or less formal Anglo-Saxons. The success of the "best company to work for" scheme in the United Kingdom is evidence on this point. What is also interesting in this context is the fact that many people who get along with their peers become more tough and less friendly after they have been selected to become managers of their old colleagues. Secondly, some managers still believe in the old-fashioned donkey methods, namely, that you have to occasionally hit the beast with a stick otherwise it will become lazy and not move forward. Or if they themselves don't favor such methods, they suspect that their boss does. I recall being surprised as a young graduate in seeing my nice American boss (who was one of the main reasons in choosing that firm) being replaced. His simple answer stays in my memory: "Well, you know, nice guys don't always win ball games." Another possible reason is that some leaders who are not very "people-oriented" think that they can achieve good results by other methods, for example, by exercising tight financial control or by elaborating a superior company strategy.

The net result of bad staff treatment has been described in several recent books. This includes a newly observed conflict between directors and managers in addition to the traditional one between directors and workers. The result also includes increasing cases of workers' extreme behavior when things get too bad such as sabotaging company equipment like internal computer systems or, worst of all, committing suicide on the premises. I understand that certain health authorities carrying out prehiring medical examinations now warn potential candidates that they are entering firms where there have been high levels of stress-related illness.

Of course, conflicts also occur at the *same* level in the hierarchy and those at the top can be very pronounced, although they are rarely made public. During a spell as secretary to the board in a fairly large UK company, I was able to witness firsthand the various conflicts that can take place between the chairman, the managing director, and the other directors. It was extremely difficult to stay factual and neutral both during these sessions and in the written proceedings of the meeting that I eventually had to produce, but anything else would have made me liable to lose not only the secretaryship but also my job in the company. Hence a piece of advice to readers: Unless you want to take the risks to fight to get to the top, it may be preferable to stay at senior management level, competently doing your work and avoiding political conflicts that can otherwise easily lead to your dismissal.

Communication

Personal communication skills have already been discussed in the skills section of chapter 2. Here we will be discussing *organizational* communication.

Within the organization, communication will be flowing from the boss down and from below back up to the boss. This communication may be formal and frequently written or informal and verbal. In most Anglo-Saxon firms, communication tends to be more informal than within continental European firms.

As an example, while working in California as a research engineer, I had to make a presentation to the company president—a person several layers above me in the hierarchy. At coffee time afterward, I asked him, "Did you find my presentation useful, sir?" "Yes, very good," he replied, "but don't call me 'sir.' Call me John." Now, in a European firm, one would not even call one's direct boss by his first name, never mind the company president. In a Swiss research organization that I once visited, the staff members would stand up and say, "Good morning, sir" like in the military whenever their boss entered their office.

On the question of downward communication, staff members often complain that they are not informed about important things or only informed once all the decisions have been taken. In one particular situation, an external project manager had been working in secret to arrange the merger of one business unit with another. When he finally presented the project to the staff, there was a big uproar and several things were brought out that had never been considered. In the end there was so much resistance that the whole idea had to be dropped.

Regarding upward communication, the boss wants to be informed as to what is going on at lower levels in the firm. However, many bosses do not like to hear bad news, and this can lead to a climate of fear whereby problems tend to remain hidden.

A serious situation arose in a British firm where I was working in that a piece of equipment began producing a high proportion of faulty products but no one stopped the machine because that would affect unit production costs, and no one dared tell the boss about the problem. When I learned what was happening and informed the boss (a risky thing to do), and he finally ordered a halt in production, customers had already installed hundreds of these products. As many of these products began to fail during usage, customers were naturally furious; they required our staff to remove the whole batch, replace them by similar products (bought from a competitor!), and cancelled future contracts with us. This one episode cost the firm 20% of its annual profit and illustrates the serious consequences of a "problem-avoiding boss."

We could contrast this behavior with the edict of Howard Geneen who so successfully managed the ITT communications conglomerate for many years. He would forgive you for any problem as long as you brought it to his attention at the first available weekly meeting.

Turning now to external communication, we often find a false image given to the public that does not at all correspond to the situation inside the organization. This can cause new recruits to come into the firm and become unhappy soon after their arrival. In one particular case during a cocktail party to welcome a new staff member, I felt a great pity when he made a speech saying how much he looked forward to working in that particular job. Sure enough, he soon discovered what the situation was really like and tried to change things a bit too obviously; within a year he was fired.

The above story emphasizes the need for every candidate to find out what it is really like to work in an organization before he signs his contract; this can only be done by having a good friend already working there with whom one can have a serious talk—off the premises, of course. The other major criterion is getting along well with your boss. Presumably, this becomes obvious at the interview but is no guarantee of the long-term contentment: One of my personal misfortunes was several times having my friendly boss transferred to another position within a few months of my appointment (hopefully not as a punishment for hiring me).

The same kind of thing often happens with annual reports: There is invariably a section saying how much the firm has appreciated the contribution of the staff and workers. This is extremely irritating to read if, as in many cases, the firm treats their staff poorly.

Another example is when the firm is communicating with the press. Possible ideas for the future are frequently presented as projects that are already in the course of realization. Future forecasts or objectives are presented seriously even if they are quite ridiculous.

In a recently published press article, an organization was trying to persuade local authorities to provide some financial assistance that would enable it to progress to be one of the five best in the country (it was then around 20th). If we blame their spokesman for making such an unrealistic statement, what should we think of the highly placed people who seemed to believe it? Why did they not ask for details as to how this could possibly be done and whether the 15 in-between competitors would themselves be making no progress during this time?

Delegation

In today's tough business climate with minimum staff, managers are swamped with work that they can't delegate because there is no one to delegate to. This is quite a change from the easygoing 1960s when many managers could build up their empires and have a nice life themselves.

In one organization that I joined, the market research department at headquarters consisted of no fewer than 20 people. The manager in charge was always available for a friendly discussion or a pleasant lunch. A few years later, when things became tougher, the size of the department was reduced to five people, which really seemed sufficient for the work needing to be done.

Of more interest for this study are cases of delegation that went wrong. Thus, in one business school, the graduate program manager delegated the recruitment of MBA students to his assistants. Although there had been many initial inquiries, very few of these were converted to definite applications after the interview process. The total numbers were finally so low that the program had to be cancelled and the program manager claimed that this was due to the difficult recruitment climate at that time. Having myself run an MBA program for a couple of years, I knew the importance of having the candidate meet with the highest possibly ranked staff—ideally myself and the dean. As well as being in a better position to answer all their questions, the MBA student, who is normally a very demanding person, was made to feel much more important by the presence of high-level people at his interview.

A very similar situation in the international context occurred during a mission sent by the business school to look for students in India. The team of two people were both relatively young, one of them being a woman. Unfortunately, no one had taken into account that the people who would be most credible and respected in that country were older men having considerable experience and an established academic background.

Controlling

It is appropriate to discuss control separately for different types of organizations. Beginning with small firms, their chief problems at launch concerns having a team with some experience and sufficient start-up capital.

Assuming they have calculated their break-even point and prepared an initial budget, their main ongoing concern will invariably be that of cash flow; stocks and debtors will need to be constantly surveyed, particularly as some of the debtors may go out of business.

In larger firms, preparation of budgets and long-term plans will have become a habit. Financial ratios will be examined and all aspects of continuous activity will be closely monitored together with the profit and loss statement. Their recent problems have been more related to high debt on the balance sheet resulting from overambitious projects or investments like acquisitions. A third category of organization is a privately run institution, one having public subventions or support (e.g., in the area of higher education). Control in these types of units tends to be rather lax, not exceeding the annual budget being the main constraint. While keeping a close watch on the smallest staff expenses, the directors in such places have no qualms about their own travel, expensive lunches, or arranging frequent receptions in the institution. In one situation that I came across, they even arranged for the departure of their financial controller who was getting a bit too familiar with these practices.

Of course, the financial crisis affecting everyone in 2009 will make control much more severe everywhere. There are even reports on the curtailing of farewell drinks for staff who are departing after many years of service.

We now turn to the new section that has been introduced here concerning *external control*. It is obviously a very topical subject since much of the blame for the current financial crisis is now being put on the shoulders of ineffective control institutions.

Restricting ourselves here to the microenvironment around a company, we have had all kinds of groups in place like auditors, administrative or supervisory boards with nonexecutive directors, accreditation agencies, and so on, but this has not always prevented financial scandals of varying degrees of magnitude.

What is amazing in these situations is that all parties will claim their ignorance as to what was going on. Now, assuming that most people would not deliberately associate themselves with fraud, it suggests that they really didn't know, or, if they had any suspicions, they would refrain from pursuing them further. The people in the first category are certainly incompetent since, in many cases, everyone from the security guard upward knows that something wrong is going on. The people in the second category, which probably represent the majority, behave in this way because we have created a "scratch-my-back society": "We will continue to use your services as long as you don't cause us any problems." Most individuals who appreciate the prestige of sitting on these bodies and earning attendance fees are quite happy with this kind of arrangement.

Not having had any personal experience within scandalous company situations, I will restrict myself to some comments about the work of certain external bodies that have relationships with business schools.

My first example concerns accreditation agencies that collect fees for granting and maintaining the accreditation of the institution—an increasingly important factor for determining the ranking of the school and hence the quality and numbers of students that it is able to attract. What has perturbed me about the accreditation procedures is their choice as to what is really important. Some years ago we had to revamp and modernize our MBA program, and I was very pleased with the course content that we finally agreed upon. However, during the meeting with the accreditation team, we were asked all kinds of questions about learning objectives and outcomes and virtually nothing about the contents of the courses.

Similarly today, the agencies have decided that the key requirement is research. Schools are therefore hiring lots of postdoctorate candidates who can produce many academic papers, even though most of these people have had almost no industry experience, and many are rather feeble in teaching abilities. Since probably no more than 10% of academic non-scientific papers have much value in business activity, I wonder if this is really the right priority to pursue—assuming of course that lecturers do keep up to date in the lecture material that they offer. Curiously, books are not as highly valued as academic papers in these procedures even though, obviously, books must be very useful—otherwise no editor would want to publish them.

Then there is the case of agencies that were called upon to award quality certification to teaching institutions. As they did not have the knowledge and experience of what was really important there, they based their procedures on what they had developed for companies. One of the elements on which they placed great importance was the satisfaction of the client, who they rather naïvely assumed was the student. This is a totally incorrect supposition since in a business school, the "client" is a combination of the student, the parents (or whoever pays the fees), and the student's future employer. In addition, the student's work must meet the requirements of the diploma-awarding institution—a point that was difficult to accept by one of our executive MBA students who was paying his own fees. In fact, the only clear-cut example of a client is when a company asks the school to provide some in-house training for their staff.

Thus, we have alternate directives at the two extremes: one favoring the production of research papers and the other blindly wanting to satisfy all student demands. Surely an intermediate, balanced position is what is ideally required.

Finally, what is very striking is that the accreditation procedures take little account of the quality of management running the school. If they did, then maybe many of the points discussed here would not exist.

Miscellaneous Operating Activities

As some commonly performed activities don't fall neatly under any one heading of a management process, they will be discussed here.

Coordination

This topic, linked to communication and (devolved) organization, is a frequent cause of management problems. We have heard about situations in some firms where marketing—trying to best satisfy their customers—does not coordinate well with production (trying to minimize their variety and costs), so that there is either too little or too much suitable material in stock.

A recent, if relatively minor, personal example comes from a business school where I regularly taught a group of around 40 students. The course seemed to be popular so that other program managers were permitted to send their students there also. Arriving one morning, I found 70 people, many sitting on the floor in a room that had a maximum capacity of 50 people. As there were no larger rooms available at that time, the first lecture session (in a fairly short 18-hour course), had to be cancelled.

Ecological pressures are now often enhancing these problems, such as the production of a low water–consuming washing machine that doesn't clean well or (to use the example of a personal battle I faced with a supplier) a low energy–consuming fridge whose internal temperature will not fall below 10° C. In short, people working in their own narrow sphere pay little attention to the consequences on others. This kind of behavior needs to be changed or suitable coordinators be appointed to control it.

Meetings

Meetings often occupy as much as half of a manager's time and are a common cause of complaint. This is partly because of the tendency to call meetings of several people where a simple discussion between the two or three main parties concerned would be sufficient. I have come across leaders who would invite participants unable to make any contribution to the discussion, simply in order to have a sufficiently large audience to listen to their own words of wisdom.

The next point concerns ignorance of how to run the meetings. Notes and even books are now available to indicate the various formalities required in a meeting: minutes, agenda, participation, and so forth, but what is most important is the control exercised by the person leading the meeting as to how much discussion should take place on each item while giving everyone an opportunity to express their views.

Another common failing is to start the meeting talking about trivial things that take up so much time that there is an insufficient amount of time left for a thorough discussion of the really important matters. An effective meeting starts off with a communication portion, followed by a presentation of problems or opportunities that have been studied by working parties. There then follows the discussion at the end of which there is a decision-making phase (as previously described in the decision-making section of this text). The execution of agreed decisions is a responsibility then given to named persons who will be called upon to report progress at future meetings.

Resources

It is normal that managers never have enough resources to do all what they would like to do. The first step in overcoming this handicap is to grade their proposed activities in terms of importance and subsequently to allocate the most resources and effort to the things that are most important. This type of approach is not only essential for managers under pressure but also very beneficial for students and almost everybody else, yet it is amazing how few people actually practice it.

A natural extension of this principle is that, if you lack the resources for a new activity, you should consider whether some other activity can be stopped because it is no longer needed and its resources should be transferred to your present needs. When I once mentioned this possibility in a meeting, the leader asked his next-door neighbor as to what I was talking about.

Blaming the Workers

When some aspect of operations goes wrong, it is tempting to blame it on the (first line) workers. Of course, workers, like everyone else, can make mistakes, but in the vast majority of cases the original fault lies with the management.

Before blaming the worker, it is essential to first consider whether he or she

- has been suitably selected and trained in the correct procedures to perform the work,
- has been given a realistic task that is achievable in the required time and up to the required quantity and quality standards,
- has been provided with sufficient resources (human, equipment, information, etc.) to carry out the task.

All of these factors are managerial duties, and in most cases it is the failure of the manager that is responsible for the problem that eventually occurred.

Culture and Past History

In our discussion about the quality of managers, it is clearly impossible to completely separate the manager from the firm in which he is working. One important aspect within the firm is its culture and some firms have a much more distinctive culture than others. The GE company is well known for its particular culture, which is appreciated by some but not by others. When the lighting firm where I used to work was taken over by GE, some of my old colleagues made career progress, but others were not so happy and left. One of the clear-cut examples of the effect of culture was the case of soccer coach Paul Le Guen who led Lyon to win several consecutive French championships and lately did well at the PSG club in Paris. In between these two, however, he had a spell with Glasgow Rangers, also a very good club, which was a complete disaster—obviously the culture there was too alien for him even though the French are supposed to get on well with the Scots!

The past history of the firm will also have a big influence on the performance of the new manager. Taking again the case of GE, it was obviously very hard for Jeff Immelt to follow the legendary Jack Welch, for many years voted best company manager in the United States. How could he improve on the excellent performance that Welch had realized during his time of office? However, there are far worse situations in which new entrants can find themselves. I think of the examples of rather unscrupulous managers who come into a company with the main objective of improving their resume so that they can subsequently get a more attractive job elsewhere. To do this they cut down on investment in everything ranging from advertising to new equipment and research. The company therefore shows a great profit improvement during their period of office but of course their successor is left with an unenviable situation to put right, however good a manager he might be.

Strategic Elements

Strategy is a favorite topic for business school students and a sought after activity for a large number of company advisors and consultants. How is it then that despite all this available assistance, so many problems arise to companies through either pursuing the wrong strategy or of badly implementing it?

Research has shown that strategic problems mostly occur during or just after major change points such as acquisitions or other large projects. Why were such projects undertaken? Principally because of the requirement of growth—in financial terms for the shareholders and in all aspects for company heads wanting to demonstrate their dynamism and to enhance their reputation with the media and the business world.

(Numerous other leaders also achieved good results through continuous and steady growth but they were rarely talked about.)

It is only in recent years that the alternative concept of "optimize rather than grow" began to be accepted. On this particular point I recall making a proposition to a business school that instead of increasing student numbers too quickly, they should first aim for excellence in pedagogical quality (in which they were already quite good), as this would attract the best students and enhance the school's reputation. This idea seemed too strange to them at that time, so they continued on an expansion route to the point where eventually 25% of the annual student intake should probably not be there. The school ranking continued to decline and it will now be hard to reverse the trend.

I would suggest that the companies that follow the optimization route will be in better shape to handle the massive fall in demand during the present financial crisis, and a new type of manager may well be about to emerge to pilot this kind of situation.

Apart from the excessive pursuit of growth, what other errors did the company leaders commit? They did not pay enough attention to consumer desires being modified by the changing macroenvironment in areas like pollution, health, energy conservation, in the advent of market saturation for certain products, in the greatly increasing share being taken by the fast-growing, less-developed countries.

Finally, a major link of this subject to the management processes discussion is in terms of control. Whereas most aspects of operations can be adequately controlled, strategy is hardly controlled at all. It is only through the actions of a few brave independent individuals on company boards that certain elements of strategy can be modified and, as we have discussed previously, this does not work often enough in practice.

Technical Skills, Functional Skills, and Emphasis

I always believed that a person working in a certain function or in a certain industry needed a reasonable knowledge of that activity. However, this view was not shared by many in Anglo-Saxon countries where they asserted that "good raw material" could be trained to do almost any job.

Thus, for example, while working in the lighting industry, I had a boss who had a university degree in botany. When we were once discussing electronic controls, I had some difficulty in following the details despite my original degree in the engineering field; I really wondered how much of the conversation he could understand.

Similarly, we had a contact in the subsidiary of an American electrical tools company who had just appointed as managing director a person whose previous post was that of sales director in a ladies garment firm. It would be quite impossible for a person without a science or engineering degree to become head of a German electrical company. Similarly in France, everyone has to have an appropriate diploma—people say jokingly that even a cleaning lady will soon need one!

On the subject of functional skills, every person should have built up an expertise in at least one area, be it in marketing, finance, production, or other. Working in the planning field after a general MBA, I was able to meet the greater requirement of knowing something about all of them and the same is really demanded of a general manager (GM).

We were once amused to receive an application for GM of one of our transport subsidiaries from a person who had nothing but marketing experience; when asked how he would manage to deal with problems in other functions, he simply replied that he would pass them on to the respective managers. Nevertheless, this kind of situation is still found among leaders. A past study asserted that there were five types of leaders, each type using mainly a single function (obviously one that they most appreciated) to drive the company. Thus, they would base their leadership on strategy, human resource management, control, change, or technical expertise. In my opinion, all of these may need to be used at different times to a greater or lesser extent.

There is a similar situation in the case of the key aspects of emphasis for the company's successful operations. For many it is quality, for Jack Welch in his last years it was speed of response, but again, I don't think it is possible to concentrate so much on one of them as to ignore others. Thus, I was horrified in seeing a video a few years ago in which the then head of Motorola said that as far as he was concerned, efficiency did not matter—it was only excellent service to the customer that was important!

Conclusions: Why Do We Have Bad Managers?

Let's make it clear at the outset that by *managing* we're talking about someone who is managing people as well as tasks and thus individuals working solely by themselves will not be included.

So the first obvious reason is that some people have been hired or selected as managers who are lacking the inherent people skills for that function—particularly such skills as motivating, coaching, or handling conflict with others. In some cases, these skills can be instilled by effective management development, but for certain people even that will not succeed.

Thus, for example, competent specialists in their field like salespersons can be wrongly promoted to become sales managers while not having the skills to manage others. This will have a doubly negative effect in that the firm acquires a bad manager and at the same time loses a good salesperson. This is also a common criticism made against many MBA graduates today. In fact business schools do a disservice to their students by suggesting that they will all become managers on graduation; possibly two out of three will, the rest will sometimes act as team leaders or become individual specialists, which can still provide them with a satisfactory career (see Figure 3.1).

A second reason is that they have been appointed as managers without sufficient experience of working in a company and handling diverse situations. This feature can also include "nonaction" people who have never created or run any activity. To make up for this deficiency, business schools insist on a substantial period of internship and look for evidence of running some form of student association or of having organized some type of significant event.

The lack of a business education can be a handicap to a prospective manager if he or she lacks the analytical skills typically developed within a business school curriculum. Such a person may therefore rely too much

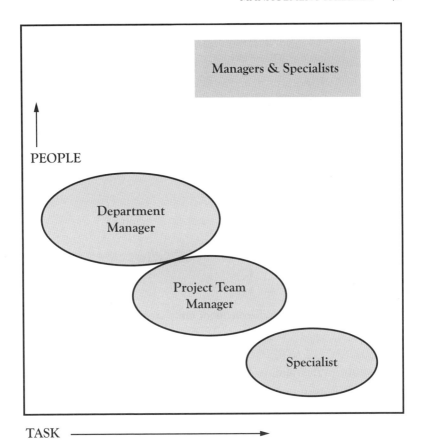

Figure 3.1. Managers or specialists.

on subjective feelings and intuition without adequately evaluating all possible alternatives, each with their particular advantages and constraints.

Not being sufficiently familiar with the five management processes will also be a handicap to them. The fact that many of these "autodidactes" (as they say in French) often possess lots of drive, experience, or intuition does not always make up for the other shortcomings.

These points are illustrated in Figure 3.2, which compares the overall rating of a recent business graduate (12 out of 20) with an experienced self-made entrepreneur (14 out of 20). Obviously, a good manager who can combine the attributes of both types can achieve the highest scores (16 out of 20 or more).

Competencies		Actions	
Innate plus Experience		Motivating Others	
5		5	
Formal Education		Doing Oneself	
5		5	

Self-taught entrepreneur

4	5		
1	4	=	14/20

Well-educated graduate

3	2		
4	3	=	12/20

Ideal manager

4	4		
4	4	=	16/20

Figure 3.2. Self-made, well-educated, and "ideal" managers.

If we accept the validity of this analysis, how can one explain that bad managers still exist among those who seem to possess all the necessary requirements? I suggest that there are two reasons for this.

The first should be obvious to all of us who have learned a foreign language at school—if it is subsequently not practiced, it will be forgotten. It is essential, therefore, to constantly practice management techniques until they become automatic. A simple way to do this is to start off by analyzing it in terms of the planning, organizing, leading or controlling elements each time we have a reasonably complicated activity to perform.

The second reason is more complex and has hardly been recognized. It arises from a lack of personal introspection whereby the manager is not correcting his weak skills nor adjusting his intrinsic behavior to meet the needs of a particular situation. For example, we could quote a person who normally likes to avoid detail or one who by nature has an extroverted and tough personality. Sometimes these inherent tendencies have to be modified in order to achieve the best results, just as one would adjust between autocratic and democratic behavior. Figure 3.3 illustrates some of the extremes between which one may need to adjust.

Factor	Extremes
Role of the Enterprise	Social Responsibility ....Profit Maximization
Alternative Orientations	Human ....Task
Type of Leadership	Democratic .... Authoritarian
Approach to a Problem	Broad & Generalized .... Narrow & Detailed
Communication	Informal .... Formal

Figure 3.3. Positioning between extremes.

These reasons are what could be described as "generalized" reasons. To these we can now add more specific reasons relating to failings in particular processes or skills. The following list consists of a selection that emanated from the cases studied in this chapter; others might wish to modify it or add further items:

- Poor staff selection and unsatisfactory performance evaluation
- Inadequate staff motivation and level of respect
- Insufficient or less than truthful communication
- Delegation of certain key tasks to the wrong people
- Poorly handled decision-making process
- Lack of balance between reflection and execution
- Inconsistency between amount of effort and degree of importance
- Insufficient evaluation of the 3Rs for new projects (realism, resources, and returns)
- Not adapting planning targets to increasingly rapid changes in environment
- Not keeping close control (and quickly correcting problems)
- Avoiding necessary change or making changes too frequently
- Inadequate understanding of all management functions (for GMs)

CHAPTER 4

Ideal Managers and Excellent Companies

Ideal Managers

Chapters 2 and 3 have indicated numerous criteria that can be used to assess good managers. This section of chapter 4 analyzes two examples of universally recognized good managers and, subsequently, proposes a new method of rating such managers over a long-term period of their careers.

For several years the press has been publishing lists and rankings of best managers. The *Financial Times'* listing of respected managers is one of the best known; it is based on surveys of a large number of executives in all kinds of companies around the world.

For a long time, Jack Welch of General Electric (GE) was selected as being the number one manager in the world. This choice was invariably due to his excellent record in continually increasing profits and market capitalization of his firm over a period of around 15 years. However, one cannot help but feel that this was self-sustaining public relations, because other managers who had less media attention and longer periods of increasing profits were largely ignored. After he retired from GE, Jack Welch worked on a book published under the title of *How to Win*. In the book he lists the eight key factors that he found most important while running GE. These have been paraphrased into the following form:

1. Set and transmit vision and goals
2. Establish strong, positive company culture
3. Select and develop top team
4. Give an example of frankness, optimism, and energy
5. Combine learning and instinctive action
6. Make and execute decisions, even if unpopular

7. Take risks but assume responsibility

8. Celebrate success

To comment on this list, one would say that the contents seem rather random compared to what has been indicated in chapters 2 and 3. Several of the items (vision, culture) can only be decided by top leaders and are thus not relevant to middle or even senior managers. Proceeding by instinct and taking risks is also only valid for people having a lot of past experience and being high up on the company ladder. Many of the personal items are very particular to the character of Jack Welch himself and may not be transposable to someone else. In order to better assess some of these qualities, my students and I have been analyzing videos of Jack Welch and of another highly rated chief executive, the Frenchman Vincent Bolloré, elected by his peers as French businessman of the year in 1989. His family firm, founded in 1822 in Brittany, is now one of the top 500 companies in the world as a diversified enterprise in sectors like transportation, distribution, packaging, and media.

Bolloré shares many of Welch's eight key items, but there is an immense contrast in their respective attitude toward people. Welch fostered a close relationship with his managers—especially the best 20%—but kept a distance to with the weakest 10% of staff who were encouraged to leave and go elsewhere. Bolloré could be tough on poorly performing top managers, but he respected, motivated, and rewarded (above average norms) all his staff who had shown him immense loyalty and made salary sacrifices during difficult times—which were later repaid.

While Welch felt justified making 30% of the workers redundant in order to maintain a profitable subsidiary for the other 70%, Bolloré tried to keep all his workers even if reducing their salaries and company dividends until times got better. "Work is made for man and finance is there to serve industry" rather than the reverse, he was quoted as saying.[1]

These contrasts are partly explained by the differences in business culture between the United States and continental Europe; the latter encourages the spread of rewards more evenly between the various stakeholders (shareholders, managers, workers, local community), while the United States favors the first two at the expense of the others. Bolloré

---

1. Quotes 1 and 2 are from TV programs *Business Matters* broadcast by the British BBC network

tried not only to conserve jobs but also to keep them in the same location so that staff members did not have to be uprooted from their locality; in the United States, workers have learned to live with such predicaments.

There are, however, notable exceptions. One can cite the case of Harley-Davidson (HD): when cutting back 40% of its workers, it assured them of a return if the company recovered, which it did. Also, the HD decision not to close down the Pennsylvania manufacturing factory (to transfer it to the Millwake site) saved the economy of the local community, as well as avoiding many redundancies and greatly improving workers' morale and productivity, which probably made up for the extra costs of retaining the two sites.

Regarding strategy, Welch's requirements of 15% annual growth and to be first or second in the market (or be sold) were not tenable in the long term. The industrial base of GE was thus continually reduced in favor of services. However, it was not appropriate to try to manage their acquisitions in all sectors—especially the NBC media company in exactly the same way as the others and this caused great resentment and departures from its staff. Similarly, the GE finance arm will need to adapt drastically to the post-2008 world crisis situation, which is already affecting it.

Like many other firms in the late 1990s, Bolloré overextended himself with acquisitions and debt, which badly affected his profits for a few years. Since then, the financial holding company he created has been in good health, and he has also moved into media services. His investment in batteries for electric cars is a laudable move, which will hopefully still prosper once the big automobile firms also move into the same market.

One of the key factors to emanate from this discussion is that big company chiefs mostly occupy themselves with different aspects to those of the managers who are effectively "running the show." "I am really just an overhead here and don't do very much,"said Jack Welch. Having put in place a company vision, culture, and overall strategy, it is Welch's managers who handle the daily management processes, consulting him only regarding decisions on the bigger issues. Although also delegating a lot, Bolloré does get somewhat more involved with day-to-day matters as evidenced by his walkabouts and chats with individual factory workers.

This special behavior of leaders was brought out previously in chapter 2, which showed that their main management activities were those denoted by vision, culture, and strategy (plus communication, motivation, and change).

The distinction should be carefully noted, but as there are many more man-agers than company chiefs, it is still important also to carry out the other management processes according to the principles given in chapter 2.

Possible New Rating Procedure

Two weaknesses of the *Financial Times'* best-manager lists and those in other publications, were that (a) they were based on worldwide executive surveys so that managers with little media coverage tended to be ignored and (b) they were a snapshot in time rather than an assessment over the lifetime of the person concerned.

For an example of the first weakness, one could cite Charles Knight of Emerson, who, despite 27 years as the head of a firm that continuously raised sales and earnings, was not listed in these publications. Regarding the second weakness, a good example is Wedeling Wiederking of Porsche, who was very highly rated before falling through overconfident and risky actions.

The assessment proposed here is therefore to rate these managers on a scale from A downward, giving an A rating only to people who have shown excellence over their whole preretirement career. It would therefore include not only "stars" like Welch and Gates but also people like Knight and, on a somewhat smaller scale, British Imperial College graduate Wilf Corrigan, who grew LSI Logic through several stages to nearly $2 billion sales with-out any significant setbacks (even though in the United States, unlike in Europe, one's career is not compromised by a single failure).

Among possible future promotions to an A grade would be regularly cited managers (now to be placed on a B rating), like Richard Branson of Virgin and Steve Jobs of Apple—provided they continued to avoid major errors, which could have them relegated to a C.

Merely satisfactory managers (probably a majority) would be rated D and the poor ones an E (it is amazing how many of the latter manage to survive in their firm—or even find jobs elsewhere).

The final category F would range from the very bad down to those even accused of corruption.

As these previous assessment grades are similar to those used in many business schools, they should hopefully find favor among the student and academic research community.

Excellent Companies

The performance of a company is linked to the character of its top manager, so it is not surprising that the separate *Financial Times* lists of the best managers and best companies have a close relationship, for instance, Welch and GE or Gates and Microsoft (Toyota, IBM, and Coca-Cola were the other regular top listed firms). However, a more realistic evaluation of companies requires an independent and suitably focused assessment. To do this, it is first necessary to identify the key factors that are important to take into consideration. From the numerous studies that have been made during the past two decades, one can synthesize eight significant factors as follows:

- Vision and culture
- Leadership and strategy
- Innovation in products
- Processes and systems
- Human resource management
- Delivering product and service to market
- Customer satisfaction
- Financial performance
- Environment and social responsibility

(*Fortune* magazine often went further by trying to select the best and worst companies under *each* of these categories. In 1999 Enron was the top of their list for innovation and quality of management—which just goes to show how difficult it is to know exactly what is going on inside a company.)

The majority of studies that try to identify the best companies were based on mainly *one* of these criteria—the most common one, which also happens to be most easily calculated, being financial performance. This could be in terms of a wide range of parameters such as profit growth, increase in market capitalization, or total stockholders return. Others tend to focus on customer satisfaction—normally a laudable approach but unfortunately many firms rated highly on this factor tend to treat their workers and suppliers rather poorly.

However, most of the nonfinancial assessments tended to stress the great importance of people management. Thus came about surveys based on the concept of "best companies to work for," which is popular particularly in the United States and the United Kingdom. Most of the companies on their lists tend to be in services—professional services like consultants, retail services, but also some research and high-tech firms like Google and Genentech. They are characterized not only by the facilities that they provide to the staff but also by the whole way in which people are treated, trained, and rewarded. Evaluations of these companies indicate that they can sometimes also perform twice as well as some of their nonlisted rivals. This is not surprising bearing in mind the high cost of staff turnover and labor disruptions. Take as example the Agro firm of Rouillier in Brittany, France, which reached €2 billion turnover in 50 years without having had a single strike!

To accommodate the diverse views regarding the relative importance of the various factors (particularly emanating from the two extreme camps: financial and people), it became necessary to devise composite indices that included several parameters. Moreover, it was considered appropriate to subdivide them into two categories, essentially representing the "end" and the "means." By "end," we refer to the effectiveness of the company in achieving its objectives; "means" are the methods by which this has been achieved. In the list of eight parameters, there would thus be a split between the first five and the last three.

This approach was widely accepted and has formed the basis for analyzing companies in the United States by the Baldridge method and in Europe by the European Foundation for Quality Management (EFQM) method.

The parameters finally selected by EFQM as shown in Figure 4.1 are divided equally between "enablers" (means) and "results" (ends). In addition each one is given a percentage weighting toward a total of 100%.

From the weightings (the equivalent Baldridge parameters are shown in brackets), it will be seen that there is a close correlation between the two approaches for all parameters except the "business results." Not surprisingly, it was to be expected that the American figure would be higher but not quite to the extent of 45% versus 15%.

Baldridge and EFMD thus evaluate a candidate company on the total score obtained in such an assessment and, in my opinion, this is the best method so far devised to determine the degree of excellence of a

---

2. Two students under my supervision wrote master's theses using this approach: one on a chocolate manufacturer in France, the other on a group of automobile components firms in Poland. The latter was graded top student of the year.

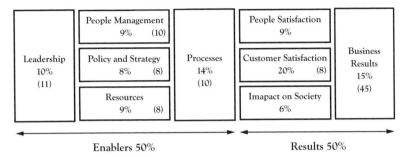

Figure 4.1. EFQM overall quality assessment for companies.

company.[2] However, it is suggested that a minimum hurdle be adopted for within each parameter so that none can be insufficiently counted.

There remains of course the need to secure agreement as to what parameters should be selected and what weighting should be accorded to each. In the 2009 situation it seems essential to bring in an ecology parameter representing at least 10% of the total. This could be taken out of the 20% customer element in the EFQM model and out of the 45% in the Baldridge model—the original figure being quite unrealistic in the present context of the world economic situation.[3]

Baldridge and EFQM do not widely publicize their "winners"—many firms undertake the evaluations mostly for their own benchmarking purposes. With the ending of the *Financial Times* surveys, those which that remain tend to be too much oriented toward the United States (e.g., *Fortune*) or toward the financial side (e.g., *Barron's*). The best balance seems to be those now carried out by the Reputation Institute (RI), whose criteria are almost identical to the eight listed on the earlier page in this chapter, except that RI includes customer satisfaction within the product and service element and selects "governance" instead of vision and culture.

The top three companies in the RI 2009 survey are Ferrero chocolates from Italy, IKEA home furniture from Sweden, and consumer products from Johnson & Johnson from the United States. What is startling in their results is the much greater relative presence at the top of firms from emerging countries (especially India) compared to those from Europe and the United States. These findings suggest that firms in the West have lived for too long on their laurels and need to undertake urgent self-reexamination for the business requirements of the future.

---

[3] EFQM is shortly planning to launch a revised 2010 model.

PART II

Applications to Managing in Different Contexts

CHAPTER 5

Differences in Managing Small Businesses*

Scope

The area of small business is normally subdivided by the type of entry method used. There are four such entry methods:

- Creation by start-up
- Buying (and management buyout)
- Franchising (as franchiser or franchisee)
- Family business succession

Certain aspects of creation relating to the business plan were previously discussed in the planning section of chapter 2. Subsequent to entry, the business has to be maintained and possibly expanded, and it is this feature, following start-up, which will be mainly covered in this chapter.

Introduction

The three key factors that distinguish a small business are the following:

1. Because it is small, a small business is vulnerable to the external environment—much as a small boat would be in a storm compared to a stabilized ferry.
2. A small business is very much short of all kinds of resources.

---

*This chapter is useful for entrepreneurs after the start-up of their business and for executives who, after a period in large companies, move into small firms as creators, managers, or investors.

3. A small business is highly dependent on one person—the entrepreneur in the case of creation or the investor in the case of buying and franchising.

The analysis method used in chapter 2, treating first the environment, then the resources, then the internal situation in the firm will therefore be very appropriate.

Environment

Compared to a larger or well-established company, the small firm has few reserves to survive a period of market difficulty. It has a relatively unknown image with potential customers and an uncertain credibility with bankers and suppliers. In addition, it will invariably have a narrow product focus and a restricted customer base, thus making it vulnerable to problems encountered with one or both of these issues.

Some of these handicaps can offer certain compensation. Thus, the small firm is partly protected from market downturns by having low overheads and a low break-even point. The narrow product focus means that it can develop a strong expertise in its chosen niche. With a smaller customer base it can provide a better, more customized service to them.

Resources (and Internal Situation)

The small firm obviously lacks resources in two key areas: finance and personnel. Finance could of course be obtained but probably only with security guarantees and even then at fairly high interest rates. Personnel will be lacking both in terms of numbers and in terms of expertise since highly qualified people will be too expensive to hire.[1]

The firm tries to combat these disadvantages by focusing on features like flexibility, speed of response, rapid innovation to solve customer's problems, as well as using, to the best extent possible, the staff that it

---

[1] These items mean that usage of time is a very critical factor. In my own created research bureau, it was a luxury to spend a few hours reading in the library as the cost of this time eventually had to be made up by selling more reports. Similarly, a visiting lecturer is paid his expenses but rarely anything for his travel time, which could be as long as one day of teaching. Those who survive adequately in this way are business owners who live on the premises and do not count their working time—like many shopkeepers.

possesses. Thus, to compensate for the relatively modest salaries and limited promotion prospects, the firm will try to constitute a friendly atmosphere and a feeling of individualism and belonging. The staff will gain a wide experience by having a variety of tasks and more responsibility so that they can quickly see the results of what they have done.

The Entrepreneur

The entrepreneur's *motivations for creation* are typically the following: independence, achievement, choice of location, interesting work, financial reward, and job opportunity or security. But financial rewards may not be very great until several years after creation. And nowadays many unemployed people are using creation as the only way to find work; they will have job security as long as their firm survives.

Personal Qualities

Personal qualities required to start a small business include an ambition and will to win, self-confidence, a high level of energy and work input, rebound and mental toughness in the face of difficulty, and some competence in running a business . . . but a traditional business education is not essential.

Risks and Problems

The risks and problems of starting a small business that one should be aware of beforehand include a high level of stress or a feeling of solitude (if you have no partners), a restricted private life, a possibility of financial loss, a psychological effect of failure, and an impact on your future career.

Required Skills

The required skills to run a small business are, essentially, all *interpersonal* skills; most *conceptual* skills, except, perhaps, analytical, as the newly created firm is not very complex; and *technical* skills relating mostly to expertise in the product or service being offered. Language skills are not necessary until the firm begins to export. Other valuable skills include judgment based on past experience, or intuition.

Roles to Be Exercised

From the 10 basic roles identified many years ago by Professor Mintzberg, coordinator and disseminator are hardly necessary in a small firm, and those of monitor and troubleshooter can be given to an assistant. This still leaves six roles to be performed by the entrepreneur himself—a rather tough requirement! They are the roles of figurehead, leader, spokesperson, negotiator, improver (or problem eliminator), and resource allocator.

Functional Demands

For a manufacturing business, the entrepreneur will normally have a technical background, for a service business, a marketing background. In order to greatly increase the chances of success, the entrepreneur should choose at least one partner with complimentary skills to his own. In addition, he should have access to a good accountant, a tax advisor, and a lawyer.

Self-Development

Once the firm is established, the entrepreneur will need either to hire appropriate managers or to train himself in the necessary management processes, such as planning and controlling. He should also try to improve his leadership skills and delegate as much as he can of the routine activities, giving himself more time to concentrate on future strategy, required change, and other such tasks that only he can perform.

Entrepreneurs Versus Managers

Having discussed in much detail the characteristics and behavior of a small firm entrepreneur, it is instructive to compare him with a professional manager working in a large company. This has been done in Figure 5.1 from which several contrasting elements can be identified.

Management Processes

In *planning*, the firm is following the originally established business plan and only updating it based on the real data now being obtained.

Entrepreneurs	Managers
• Creating	• Continuing
• Risk Taking	• Cautions
• Broad and Quick	• Narrower and Slower
• Individualistic	• Collective
• Own Image	• Company Image
• Power and Glory	• Professionalism
• Privileged and Secure	• Dependent and Vulnerable
• Family Links	• Business Colleague Links

Figure 5.1. Distinctions between entrepreneurs and professional managers.

In terms of *organizing*, structure is, of course, very simple and the style organic and flat. Concerning *staffing*, additional people can be hired rapidly with few formalities or written procedures.

Leading or *directing* is carried out by the entrepreneur alone, using informal communication, and methods of motivation are more diverse than found in large companies. Delegation is slowly being established to permit decision making on simpler issues to be made directly without prior reference to the entrepreneur.

There is a major emphasis on *control*, checking that actual results in terms of sales and especially cash flow are in line with business plan forecasts. More sophisticated means of control have not yet been established.

Overall, only the essential elements of management processes are being used; more sophisticated items such as strategic planning, ethics, and change management will be brought into use if the firm progresses to a larger entity. In summary (as in Figure 5.2), this informal, partial, and ad hoc approach in a new small firm contrasts with the explicit, comprehensive, and systematic process management for a larger firm, and toward which the new start-up will need to move if it develops and expands—as discussed in the following section.

Process	Key Differences for Small Firms
Planning	
• Goals	Profit more as by-product than explicit target
• Techniques:	
Start-up	Formal business plan now required
Operational	Casual, very short term
• Strategic Planning/	Rarely done
• Decision Making	Can be slow unless entrepreneur delegates
Organizing	
• Organizing Structure	Flexible roles, no charts
• Organizing Style	Informal (Organic)
• Change Management	Not yet envisaged
• H.R.M.	Ad-hoc, few written procedures
• Social Responsibility	Not high priority
Leading/ Directing	
• Leadership	By the entrepreneur alone
• Communication	Easy, informal
• Motivation	More diverse than in large companies
• Delegation	Often lacking
Controlling	
• Techniques	Partial, often ad-hoc
• Operations Control	Quality standards increasingly required
• Financial Control	Cash flow control essential
• Management Info Systems	Becoming more widely used
Overall Features	
	Informal, partial, ad-hoc *rather than* Explicit, comprehensive, systematic

Figure 5.2. Management processes in small business.

Small Business Expansion

Not all entrepreneurs want their business to grow beyond a small core of staff that they employ; they are quite happy to concentrate on their existing product or service and avoid all the complications of administration. However, for those who might eventually wish to expand, it is necessary to have at least a minimum knowledge of the procedures and consequences.

The business expansion process is very much analogous to the life of a human being going from birth to youth to adolescence and, finally, adulthood, as the firm grows from small to medium to large and very large.

During this time the role of the entrepreneur changes from being that of an owner-operator to that of an owner-manager, to that of a leader of a functionally managed organization with several layers of workers and managers. In the initial stages, his staff reports directly to him in a player and coach-type relationship; subsequently, he installs one or more levels of intermediate supervision. Thus, the firm changes from a flat or organic to a hierarchic or mechanistic style of organization.

The expansion decision itself will depend on several factors that the entrepreneur or leader will need to consider beforehand.

Firstly, is it his desire to run a bigger firm with a changed culture, partly due to the extra layers of supervision? Does he not risk "falling between two stools"—that is, losing the advantages of a small firm without gaining those of a big one? Will the eventual rewards be commensurate with the effort required?

Secondly, can he obtain the additional resources in terms of finance, suitable staff, premises, equipment, and so on? Finance will include both fixed and working capital, the latter being around 15% of the extra sales value planned.

Thirdly, can he put in place and maintain the additional operating systems like stock control, required prior to the expansion if the firm is not to be choked by a mass of data?

Fourthly, if he has to go outside for equity capital, is there a danger that investors bringing in these funds could significantly reduce his degree of control of the firm that he has created?

Finally, has he researched and evaluated the alternative possibilities for expansion like buying another firm and maybe running it as a stand-alone unit?

Only after such an evaluation has been completed can the company owner have confidence that he is making the right move.

Functions: Exporting

It is not an objective within this text to try to cover the differences in functional departments of a small business as opposed to a large one as this is a difficult task to treat in a decisive and prescriptive manner. The one exception concerns an activity within the marketing department, namely, that of exporting, which is pretty much exclusive to small firms as most of the larger ones will have created their own overseas subsidiaries.

Everyone seems to be highly in favor of exporting except approximately 80% of small firms who do not do it. Some do not even know exactly what exporting involves, but the majority see all kind of barriers and obstacles and do not think that the effort will be justified by the benefits.

In essence, the exporting sequence consists of six types of activities:

- Strategy (validity, reasons, methods, organization, resources)
- Prospection (market research, product suitability, choice of partners)
- Marketing and sales (trade fairs, catalogs, pricing, after-sales service)
- Execution of the orders (administrative tasks, documentation, contracts)
- Delivering the goods (transportation, insurance, customs)
- Payment (letters of credit, bonds, guarantees)

An important factor is the selection of the intermediary used for distribution who can be an agent, distributor, or foreign retailer, depending on the product and the conditions overseas. Note also that an export merchant can take care of many of the export procedures for firms that do not have the ability to do it themselves.

However, the most convenient solution is to have an overseas buyer come to your factory, negotiate a deal, and have him take care of all the export details. Perceived obstacles and barriers toward exporting include the following:

1. A lack of information about the foreign market and difficulties in finding reliable partners there
2. Limited resources in the firm to devote to this activity
3. Lower return on investment or even higher risks of nonpayment

There are numerous sources of possible assistance to overcome the first two of these problems including consultants, chambers of commerce, and various government agencies. A good place to start is by using the services of university students, even on an internship basis, as they have the time, the ability to find information, and some will have acquired knowledge of the required foreign language.

Exchange students will be even more valuable, as they can also help to find overseas partners, and establishing good personal relations with your overseas partner greatly reduces the risk of nonpayment of invoices.

Problems and Responses

The world of small business lives under the constant threat of failure, and the well-known rule of thumb is that half of the newly created firms will disappear within 5 years. The most common reason for failure is that the firm was "under capitalized" (lacked sufficient funds) at the time of creation. Subsequently, the firm may fail due to financial problems (especially the lack of working capital), bad market conditions, or various problems due to bad management.

In order to avoid oncoming disaster, small firms need to anticipate potential problems. A convenient method of doing this is to list potential problems under the headings frequently used in this text (macroenvironment, microenvironment, resources, and internal)—and then to think out suitable responses to each one as shown in the following example.

Source	Problem	Responses
macro environment labor law	redundancy	temporary staff
micro environment customers	bad debts	factoring
resources	new equity	secondary stock markets
internal	extra volume	exporting

Another method of reducing the vulnerability of small firms that has been developing in recent years is *networking*. This activity helps to reduce the firm's isolation and enables it to share services, information, and, in the best case, actual orders. In the following list, moving downward, we see how an isolated firm can strengthen its position, firstly on its own (items 1), secondly by participating in a network (items 2), and thirdly by linking itself closely to a larger firm (items 3).

1a	Independent in a competitive field
1b	Independent but with a strong distinctive competence
1c	Possessing a superior patented product or branded service in a very narrow niche
2a	Coordinator of operations subcontracted out to others
2b	Benefiting from shared services (e.g., intelligence, publicity, etc.)
2c	Participant within a pole of competitivity (vertical or horizontal)
2d	Member of an order-sharing network (grouped purchases or execution of part of the order)
3a	Essential contractor or partner to one important company
3b	Management buyout from a well-established business
3c	Autonomous business unit of a strong or larger company

Roles for Graduates in Small Business

As this text is aimed jointly at the academic and business community, it is appropriate to treat a subject that concerns them both. The comments that follow are based on a research project carried out a few years ago by the author for which a summary is provided in Figure 5.3.

One of the objectives was to assess in which activities (creation, maintenance, expansion, etc.) could different types of graduates (general, language, business) contribute to the management of the small business. As indicated by the "stars" allocated in Figure 5.4, it was estimated that young business graduates having also taken small business management

It seems that everyone today is praising the virtues of small business while record numbers of students are going into higher education. There is therefore an obvious tendency to direct new graduates away from their traditional first employment areas of large companies and public sector organizations into working for — or even creating, small firms. Unfortunately, as recent surveys confirm, there is at the same time a lack of appreciation for Small Business owners of what contributions graduates can make their firms; equally, a lack of recognition by graduates as to where they can fit into these structures. This project has been undertaken to address what are felt to be the major causes of this problem, in other words, an insufficient understanding of the complexities of small business situations and of the variety of competencies if different types of graduates.

Figure 5.3. What roles for graduates in small business?

The methodology of the study therefore develops a detailed segmentation of small firm situations (e.g., creation, maintenance, development) and of different types of graduates (e.g., technology, language, business majors) related to their competencies and motivations. This is then followed by a cross-analysis of small firm needs against graduate usefulness. The work is substantially based on Small Business Management courses at undergraduate and post-graduate level taught at ESC Rennes since 1992. These have included the assessment of numerous internships and over 150 business start-up plans submitted by teams of students — some of which were 'real' projects with outside partners.

After a detailed discussion of Graduate characteristics and the various small firms situations, the study draws up a semi-quantitative matrix indicating the value of each type of graduate to each kind of need. On the overall basis, the evaluations suggest that a non–graduate, << self-taught >> entrepreneur might increase his ratings score from 2 to 13 over a 15/20 year period. He is therefore not likely to be impressed (as surveys indicate), with ordinary graduates whose maximum potential score is around 6. However the Business Graduate trained in Small Business (BGSB) with his strong skills in Business Planning, Performance Monitoring, Company Growth, etc. . . . could well obtain a rating of as much as 12 points within a few years of graduation, in other words, he could become almost as a valuable an asset to the company (although of course in different areas), as the Founder/ Entrepreneur himself!

In order to optimize the development of such skills, the study draws up hypothetical career patterns for Graduates over the 25 – 40 age span. Two novel features are introduced here namely the usefulness of a spell of work with a << service provider >> to small firms, and the definition of the role of << Assistant to the Entrepreneur >> which is invariably a more realistic choice for the young graduate than a new company creation.

The main target audiences for this report are small firms, graduating students and their educators. It is hoped that it will help to improve understanding between the three parties so that increasing numbers of graduates will enter and make useful contributions to the performance of these firms.

Figure 5.3. What roles for graduates in small business?

	Creation	Aid to Creation	Maintaining	Development & Growth	Buying & Selling	Franchising	Family Succession	International	Total Score
Nongraduates	*	–	–	–	–	*	–	–	2
NG + Experience	***	–	**	*	**	**	**	*	13
Graduates	* (T)	*	–	–	–	*	*	* (L)	6
Business Graduates	*	*	**	*	*	–	*	**	9
Business Graduates With S.B. Training	**	*	**	**	*	–	**	**	12

Notes: (T) = Technology Graduate, (L) = Languages Graduate, NG = Nongraduate

Figure 5.4. Relevance of various types of graduates to different SB situations.

courses could make a comprehensive impact and almost as great in total as experienced "self-made" entrepreneurs several years their senior.

The study also identified possible career patterns (Figure 5.5) for such graduates starting off as assistants to an entrepreneur at 24 years old and involving periods of work both inside the small firm and in support organizations such as banks or chambers of commerce. Hopefully this type of research will encourage business graduates to also consider employment in small firms rather than in larger firms or consulting companies where most of them aspire to go at present.

In Company Roles	Age
Assistant to Entrepreneur	24–27
Manager (for Maintenance & Develpment)	30+
Entrepreneur or Creator	27+ / 40+
Successor in Family Firm	30+

Buyer or Franchise	35+

External Roles	Age
With Service Provider, e.g., Chamber of Commerce	24–30
With Banks/Investors	27+
As Consultant/Investor	35+

Figure 5.5. Career (and age) opportunities for graduates in small firms.

Aids for Small Firms

In many countries substantial efforts are being made to assist small firms—there are in fact too many varieties of schemes that make it very confusing for a would-be recipient.

The aid is mostly in terms of financial assistance, including loans, guarantees, exoneration from taxes, and so on. Sometimes it involves the provision of a low-rent building, including equipment and administrative services. Alternatively, it can take the form of partial payment for consultancy or market research.

Overall, the extent of financial help may represent as much as 25% of the total launch capital needed.

Most of these assistance programs relate to the creation phase, and governments like to publish numbers of new creations as an indicator of the success of their policies. Unfortunately, this creation data encompass many new firms that do not contribute very much to the nation's economy.

The majority nowadays tends to apply to people becoming self-employed because they cannot find other jobs. The question, therefore, needs to be asked: What kind of firms do we really want to create?

Among the desirable answers would be the following:

- Firms that generate new employment in addition to that of the entrepreneur
- Firms that develop new innovations, especially in sectors of high growth for the future like environmental protection and energy conservation
- Firms that will be able to export a significant proportion of their total production
- Firms that contribute to land-use planning like that of saving rural areas

It is toward those categories that most financial assistance should be directed rather than toward some of the unemployed who have idealistic projects for creating new shops, restaurants, or bars of which we probably already have enough and that cost large amounts of money in terms of space rental and refurbishing. Financial assistance, in my view, should be used to aid entrepreneurs creating useful, needed products as opposed to those designed mainly for amusement. Those people who do not fit into one of these "desirable" categories should make do with microcredit, which is now becoming more and more available, or seek private venture risk capital.

The other main focus for assisting small firms should be to minimize the number of failures of existing firms that have recently been created or in saving those created some time ago by an entrepreneur who is now going into retirement—providing of course that there is still a continuing demand for that firm's products. Very little effort or funding is at present going in this direction.

Conclusions

Even ignoring three of the four small business entry methods (buying, franchising, family business), this review has demonstrated a whole series of situations whereby small firms differ from larger companies.

Most of these are centered on the particularities of the entrepreneur, but the limitation of resources, while having to face relatively more serious threats from the external environment, also has a major impact. In a *SWOT* (strength, weakness, opportunities, threats)-type analysis, weaknesses can often be compensated by other strengths and there may be unique opportunities like exporting or by effectively using trained graduates. However, there is a constant threat of failure that requires continuous monitoring, anticipating problems, and formulating early responses to ensure survival. Some degree of network cooperation is also a very valuable safeguard.

Only a minority of people possess the characteristics to become successful entrepreneurs, but most of the rest could find satisfaction in working inside a small firm as assistants or managers—or, alternatively, in one of the many types of organizations that provide support to it.

Aid from government agencies should now be more directed toward the firms that could bring the greatest national benefits, and methods should be devised to help maintain existing small firms temporarily in trouble but that still have a promising future.

CHAPTER 6

Extra Needs for International Management*

Scope

This chapter deals with the required behavior of *executives* working for *companies* in the *international environment*. It includes a brief section on how these executives should go about developing international operations for their firms. This chapter, like the chapters before it, is skills-, processes-, and roles-oriented, leaving the movement of goods, services, capital, and labor to their separate functional departments (marketing, finance, human resource management).

Introduction

Some people have the misconception that to work internationally will only require frequent travel and learning some foreign languages. This is far from the truth; it is, in fact, like making the change from working in two dimensions (executive and company) to working in three dimensions (executive, company, country). International management requires many additional skills, a different handling of management processes, an appreciation of different roles, and an understanding as to how staff from different countries will behave.

When a company has expanded and fragmented by creating some local subsidiaries in its own country, it will already require extra effort in communication and in coordination. If these subsidiaries are in foreign

---

*This chapter is useful for those who are intending to internationalize their firm or planning a career in international business.

countries, these two items will also be different for each country concerned leading to greater complexity and greater risk.

Environment

The international environment will present a *diversity of settings* in terms of capital markets, trade union practices, legal systems, and many other factors. There will be a *variety of operating possibilities* using customers and suppliers in different countries. There will be *many cultural differences* requiring the study not only of languages but also of customs, values, and even religions. (There is also the need to take into account numerous world organizations that supervise international activities such as the International Monetary Fund [IMF], the World Trade Organization [WTO], and the International Labour Office [ILO].) Each of the three main "actors" in the process will try to impose its own demands, as is shown in the following list:

- *Countries* try to secure the maximum possible inward investment, training of their personnel, and so on.
- *Companies* look for places where they can maximize profits and minimize risk.
- *Executives* try to enhance their experience and balance allegiance between the country of their own nationality, the country where they work, and the company employing them (which may be from a yet different country).

Skills

From the previous comments we can thus begin to list the additional skills required under each of our accepted skills categories (technical, conceptual, interpersonal, and individual character).

- *Technical skills*: learning languages and customs, ensuring a high level of adaptability, experimentation, and risk-taking
- *Conceptual skills*: handling diversity as well as extra complexity
- *Interpersonal skills*: working in multicultural teams, transferring knowledge, and initiating change

- *Individual character skills*: extra mobility and ethical principles that may be different from those applied in their own country

These skills have therefore been added to the skills chart of the purely national manager (Figure 2.2) and are attached as Figure 6.1.

Processes

The *planning* process will not only need to consider the features of the different countries but will also be much more complex insofar that one has to decide what level of resources is allocated to each country, where can one find the best suppliers, where should one manufacture, how should transfers be made between the different locations, and so on.

For *decision making*, it is necessary to select what should be made centrally and what should be made locally. Also, it should be determined how they will be made, since in some countries this is done from the top down and in others from the bottom up. Moreover, certain nationalities like to participate in the decisions while other nationals do not.

The *organizational structure* of the company will of course also have to be changed, introducing location as well as product or customer or whatever system was used before. Methods of coordination will largely depend

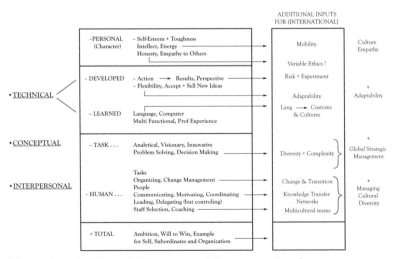

Figure 6.1. Additional skills required for international management.

on the culture and activities of the company, but company standards and procedures will need to take into account local habits.

The *staffing* procedures for local employees will obviously have to meet local regulations and could be quite different to what the company uses in its home country. Ethics can cause a major problem insofar as local practice may need to be followed to secure business even though such behavior could be illegal in the company's parent country.

The *leading or directing* process will be very much affected by the national culture; this will be understood by local managers but could cause serious problems to managers in the company's main headquarters or to expatriates sent out overseas. Appropriate methods of *communication* will need to be devised between headquarters and the foreign units and, with more difficulty, between the foreign units themselves. *Motivation* of the local employees will naturally need to follow local norms noting that in some countries, it is better to motivate the total group rather than the individual participants, also noting that motivation by financial rewards is not the best method for all nationalities.

Control is clearly more difficult and more complicated. Although the distance factor has been largely eliminated by modern computing and telecommunications, there may be concern about the reliability of financial systems and possible fraud. Decisions have to be made as to what the transfer pricing is, how much profit the overseas subsidiary should show, and what currency to use in order to minimize tax liability and reduce exchange rate risks.

In total, the additional requirements for international management are variety and complexity (VC) for planning and control and cultural diversity (CD) for leading and organizing.

Roles

It was only in 1992 that professors Christopher Bartlett and Sumantra Ghoshal elaborated the various possible roles for international managers. Apart from the obvious possibility of working in a certain function at company headquarters or in one of the subsidiaries, they identified four others, which are presented in the following list:

- *Global business management*, which is a centralized function planning and monitoring the company's activities throughout the world[1]
- *Worldwide functional management*, which coordinates the activities in the same function like technical research and engineering, in headquarters and in various overseas subsidiaries
- *Geographical subsidiary management*, which represents the general manager's role in heading the operations of a particular subsidiary
- *Top-level corporate management*, which refers to the board of directors, including the president and chief executive on the U.S. system, the chairman and managing director in the UK system, the president and Director General (DG) in France, and so on

Figure 6.2 illustrates these roles in a typical international company with three product groups and three geographical locations.

To assist students in planning a career pattern in international management, a chart has been prepared (Figure 6.3), showing possible movement between these roles as they gain in experience from around 24 years old.

In addition to these roles, one can envisage what could be called *travelling roles* during different stages of a new overseas manufacturing investment. In chronological order, these would encompass the following:

- *An investigator or negotiator* assessing possible sites during, say, 3 weeks
- *An engineer* starting up the plant during, say, 3 months
- *An expatriate* managing the facility during, say, 3 years
- *Visitors* from headquarters who come on trips of, say, 3 days

Each of these roles requires specific prior training and, for the two latter, a good understanding of the culture, habits, and acceptable behavior in the foreign country.

---

[1] Having spent most of my company career in this type of role, I would recommend it to "general" master's of business administration graduates having a reasonably good understanding of all management functions and a willingness to learn details of the firm's products. By frequent meetings with high-level operations managers and strategy-developing directors, one is constantly dealing with the company's current situation and future plans.

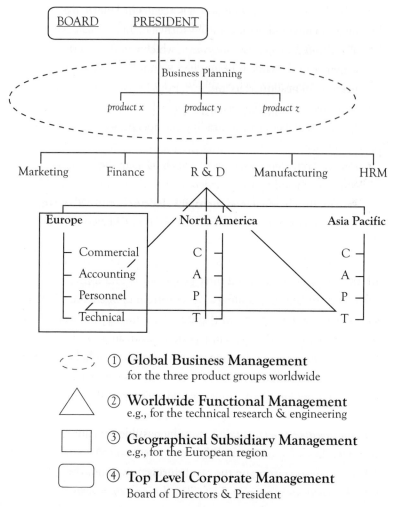

Figure 6.2. Major roles for international managers.

Comparative Management

In this section, we study the various features of managers from different countries, the purpose being (a) to anticipate how they might behave in given situations and (b) to identify the best roles that they may be able to fill. Of course, it must be remembered that we are dealing with generalities, and with globalization, these distinctions are being reduced.

		AGE
HQ Functional Dept.	–	24
Overseas Functional Dept	–	27
HQ Functional Coordination	–	30
or		
HQ Global Business Management	–	30
Geog. Subsidiary Management	–	35
Top Level Corporate Management	–	40
Chief Executive Position	–	45

Figure 6.3. Possible student career pattern in international management.

Two key aspects that are significant in this matter are the educational background of the person from his particular country and his skills portfolio in terms of strong and weak elements.

Thus, for example, the British manager could have had a degree in almost any subject as he is mostly judged on his future potential and eventual job performance. He will typically prefer to practice face-to-face informal communication and be more orientated toward people rather than detailed tasks. He will be more instinctive and subjective in his approach since he is likely to have had only limited management training. He is probably not very good in foreign languages, being comforted by the fact that English is the universal business language. On this basis, therefore, one might expect the British to be suitable as team leaders or personnel managers and, bearing in mind the previously given distinctions, thus to be more appropriate for "leadership" rather than "managership."

A comparison between the typical British manager and a French manager is shown in Figure 6.4, and a shorter list including these two plus

Aspect	French	British
Overall Label	"Bright Cadres"	Gifted Amateurs
Behavior	Measured/Progressive	Instinctive/ Entrepreneurial
Job Selection Basis Skill Pattern Favored Background	Past Diplomas Analytical/Theoretical Grand Ecole	Future Potential Pragmatic/Empirical Social Network
Outside Entry Via: Valued Training Evaluated on	Civil Service Admin/Science Degree of Expertise	Professions Accountancy/Law Job Performance
Communication Type	Written, Distant, Formal	Oral, Face-to-Face, Informal
Business Orientation	Tasks, Complexity "Managership"	People, Change "Leadership"
AREAS FOR IMPROVEMENT		
Skills/Processes	Implementation Direct Communication Internationalization	Attention to detail Objective Analysis Foreign Languages
Training Needs Middle Level	Participative Management Listening	Management Training
First Level	Public Speaking Team Leading	Tasks (Apprenticeship)

Figure 6.4. Management aspects: Comparison of French and British managers.

Germans, Italians, and small European nations like Scandinavians, Belgians, and Dutch is presented in Figure 6.5.

It would be instructive to build up the list to include not only other major nationalities such as Americans (excellent in project execution) and Chinese (renowned entrepreneurs) but also for others that at present we may only have limited information. For example, it has been said that Filipinos make good middle managers, this being partly due to the adaptability and languages that they acquired during their past colonized history.

Nationality	Educational Background	Stronger Elements	Weaker Elements	Possible Roles
• British	Often Arts/ Classics	Communication, HRM	Languages, Detail	– Team Leaders – Personal Managers
• French	Formal, Grand Ecole	Analytical, Synthesis	HRM, Implementation	– Planners – Strategists
• German	Long, Professional	Rigor, Technical	Compartmentalized Risk Aversive	– Engineers – Project Leaders
• Italian	Parochial	Flair, Entrepreneurship	Emotion, Languages	– Designers – P.R. Managers
• Belgians/Dutch Scandinavians	Multilingual	International Outlook	Leadership	– Middle Management – Expatriates

Figure 6.5. Background and functional team roles for different European nationalities.

We also need to take into account the behavior of different nationals in various management process activities. As two examples, during *meetings* the northern Europeans want to move rapidly toward a decision, while the southern Europeans insist on having their viewpoint adequately discussed. The *planning process* will be carried out differently in a firm from a country practicing a systematic and individual approach (e.g., Germany) rather than one with an ad hoc and group approach (e.g., Spain).

Another interesting aspect for comparison concerns the attitudinal positioning of different national managers regarding their behavior in the company and their objectives for the company.

In Figure 6.6, Japanese, American, British, and continental European managers are placed on a scale between the extremes of various parameters such as commitment to company versus personal life, short- versus long-term orientation, and profit maximization versus social responsibility. As might be expected, in many cases, the British are close to the Americans but it is interesting to see how the Japanese are sometimes close to the continental Europeans and sometimes to the Americans.

It is also useful to recall the functional areas in which staff from different countries or regions have tended to excel. As the first to teach business on a wide scale, the Americans have been particularly strong in finance and marketing. The Europeans excel in the areas of human resource management and engineering design. In their post–World War II development,

Attitude Positioning: British (B), Continental Europe (E), America, Japan (J)					
1. Social Responsibility	E	B	J	A	Profit Maximization
2. Long-Term Security	J	E	B	A	Short-Term Flexibility
3. Centralized	J	E	B	A	Decentralized
4. Formalized	E	J	B	A	Informal
5. Individual	E	A	B	J	Team
6. Management	J	E	A	B	Leadership
7. Diversity	E	B	A	J	Homogeneity
8. Balanced Life	E	B	A	J	Commitment to Company

Figure 6.6. Attitudinal positioning: British (B), Continental European (E), American (A), Japanese (J).

the Japanese have developed great expertise in manufacturing and statistical quality control. Finally, more recently, one can identify certain key features of Arab management based on ethics and interpersonal relations.

Developing International Operations

This brief section aims to identify the main factors to consider for developing company operations overseas. They are the following:

- What is the best strategy to pursue?
- Where is it best to invest (location)?
- What should be the extent of involvement?
- Should this be undertaken alone or with partners?

Strategy

There exist four basic strategy variations, two will be treated later and the two classical ones of "low cost" and "differentiation" now. The former is applicable to fairly standard products made in large volumes to reduce unit costs. Companies using this format are identified as global. The latter concerns products that have to vary substantially according to the country where they are sold and are the hallmark of multinational firms. A company that first goes overseas carrying out its business in its previous way (international) is thus faced with the option of moving in one direction (global) or the other (multinational).

Taking this further, in 1996 Bartlett and Ghoshal introduced the concept of a "transnational" corporation that sought to combine the best features of the two: global competitiveness and multinational flexibility, in an optimum fashion. It aimed to be a flexible integrated network with joint development and worldwide sharing of knowledge. The transition steps showing how orientation changes from home country to host country or world and then to an integrated transnational network are shown in Figure 6.7.

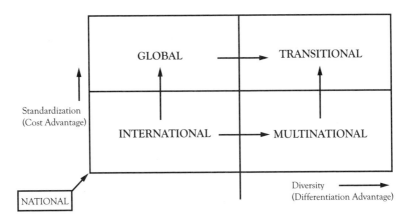

FEATURES:

INTERNATIONAL
Exploiting parent company capabilities through worldwide diffusion

GLOBAL
Building cost advantage through large scale operations

MULTINATIONAL
Achieving strong local presence by responsiveness to national differences

TRANSNATIONAL
Optimum combination

Figure 6.7. Toward the transnational: Alternative avenues of development.

Location

An assessment as to the best location for the investment needs to consider business factors such as cost of labor or logistics, but, if transfer of people is also involved, personal and cultural factors need to be taken into account as well. In addition, this evaluation will depend on the type of facility being planned be it a regional headquarters, a manufacturing plant, or a research establishment. Figure 6.8 gives an illustration of the factors to consider.

Extent of Involvement

The simplest form of international involvement is of course exporting, but in order to make a bigger and more rapid impact in the foreign

FACTOR	Headquarters	Manuf. Plant	Res. Establish
Business Factors			
• Market	✓	✓	
• Political	✓	✓	
• Economic	✓	✓	
• Labour		Avail/Qual/Prody	Knowledge workers
• Real Estate (Rent/Avail)	Offices	Ind. Sites	Science Park ?
• Infrastructure	Telecom, Airport	Road/Rail	Computer Links
• Regulations (Red tape)	✓	✓	
• Grants (Initial)		✓	✓
• Taxes (Subsequent)	✓	✓	
Personal Factors (Quality of Life)	✓	(for Managers)	✓
• Atmosphere eg. Crime	✓		✓
• Amenities eg. Schools	✓		✓
• Leisure eg. Sun, Snow	✓		✓
• Language/Culture	✓		✓
• Cost of Living	✓		
• Intellectual Excellence			✓

Figure 6.8. Overseas investment: Factors affecting choice.

country (according to the third "globalization" strategy), some foreign investment will be required. This will normally start with the creation of a foreign subsidiary that can then be extended with a manufacturing plant, a research facility, and even a full overseas division.

Alone or With Partners

Cooperation with overseas firms is the fourth of the available strategies. Exporting is usually carried out using agents or distributors who are, to some extent, partners of the firm. In a similar vein, one can consider those given a license to manufacture your product or a franchise to sell your service. On a more involved level are alliances between your firm and a foreign one for example to distribute each other's products or joint ventures like for sharing the investment in a new production facility.

Those working in international business should therefore be familiar with these different strategies and be capable of determining the optimum location, degree of involvement, and partnership options for their firm.

Conclusions

This brief review has hopefully justified the initially made assertion regarding the substantial differences in *international* management and hence the extra requirements for those who aspire to work there if they are to avoid serious mistakes and construct a successful career.

It identified the many additionally needed skills particularly those related to the leadership process in handling cultural diversity; the brief section on comparative management was an introduction to this subject that could be developed further by taking courses in intercultural management or, if need be, international negotiations.

It showed how the greater variety and complexity made business development planning, organizing, and controlling more difficult but arguably more interesting. Finally, it identified several new and different roles that staff could pursue beyond what might have been available to them in a purely national context.

PART III

Applications to External Situations

CHAPTER 7

Management Issues and Crises

Introduction

In 1998 I made a presentation at the INSEAD Business School Euro-Asia Conference considering the Asian crisis of the previous year. It identified a number of firms that had avoided the worst effects of this crisis and discussed some of the reasons why. Since that time I have periodically given lectures at various business schools on the responses that could be made to the many other similar crises that followed. In February 2008, in other words, at the time of the severe oil and raw materials price inflation, the emphasis was slightly changed to highlight "key management issues" and broadened to consider separately the challenges for nations and international organizations as well as for companies.

This chapter is a continuation of these studies and has been extended to provide some comments on the current situation subsequent to the massive financial crisis of late 2008.

Pre-2008 Crises: Trigger Points, Causes, and Effects

People today often cite the Great Depression of 1929 but seem to have forgotten the many other, albeit much less severe, crises that occurred during the past 8 years. Among them was the Internet bubble (i.e., the stock market collapse in the high-tech sector) of 2000, the U.S. recession and September 11 in 2001, the financial scandals of 2002, the launch of the Iraq War, and the severe acute respiratory syndrome (SARS) epidemic of 2003. These crises caused serious upsets in stock markets, exchange rates, and subsequently interest rates. A common factor was that nearly all of them began in the United States, but eventually the United States managed to recover from them better than the other countries that had been affected. Some things were corrected following these crises, but from what we see today, nowhere near enough was done at and since that time.

Most crises seem to arise due to either fear or greed—fear from armed conflicts, terrorism, epidemics and greed from company directors or investors wanting to get constantly higher financial rewards. The consequences are plunging stock markets and declining exchange rates that are rapidly followed by a reduced demand and the social effects of redundancy and unemployment.

Although only a very small proportion of directors were guilty of Enron-type fraud, many more enriched themselves in "allowable" ways. Others like Vivendi exhibited megalomaniac tendencies in building up huge empires, or simply making too big acquisitions like France Telecom, thus creating unsupportable debt that led to share price falls of 60% or more.

A number of companies managed to be relatively unaffected by the crisis even though their industry suffered. Among them one can cite Southwest Airlines, Toyota automobiles.

Questions and Responses for Companies—General

The salutary effect of these crises was that companies began to ask themselves fundamental questions and to consider possible responses such the following:

Why are we in business?

Factors other than simply profits began to be considered as associated goals—for example, a responsibility toward society and the new theme of "sustainable development."

What can we do best?

This led to "shrink to the core" strategies by externalizing activities of peripheral interest to the company that could perform it better or cheaper.

How do we adapt and change?

Companies began to consider optimizing rather than simply growing, giving attention to cooperation instead of investing everywhere on their own, realizing that ethical behavior and corporate governance were essential to avoid possible scandals.

How do we measure our performance?

Increasing share price would no longer be satisfactory so companies would need to consider other parameters such as shareholder value, assets to debt ratio, and so on. All of these responses can be examined more specifically according to how they were adopted by different types of organizations.

Specific Responses by Different Organizations

The following are some specific responses, which were undertaken by different types of organization:

- *Large companies*: retrenching by closing factories, delocalizing
- *Medium companies*: getting subcontracted work as large firms externalize
- *Small companies*: joining networks, seeking links to strong customers
- *Manufacturing companies*: innovative design, adding systems package
- *Service companies*: moving upmarket, stressing customer service
- *Public to private companies*: delisting to avoid shareholder constraints
- *Management consultants*: focusing on restructuring rather than acquisitions
- *Business schools*: cross-border links for a wider recognition, new courses like sustainable development

2008 to 2009 Situation

For the conference being prepared in January 2008, it was becoming obvious that issues in the international environment were becoming the dominant factors. Most of these major issues could only be treated at the national or even international level, and this will be summarized in the following tables and text.

Issues for Individual Nations

The importance of the following issues varies by country, and each country can, to a large extent, search for its own solutions:

- Concern over standard of living
- Employment, demographics, immigration
- Delocalization of manufacturing and services
- Budget deficits: health, education, housing
- Securing supplies of energy, raw materials
- Trade balance: imports and exports

Curious to find out why Germany, the most powerful economy in Europe, had the highest proportion of hard discount retailers, I discovered some disturbing statistics. Every year approximately half a million people were leaving the ranks of middle income earners to join the ranks of the poor. A key reason was that those who became unemployed lived off a series of small jobs for which there was no minimum wage, and, with low economic growth, they had little chance of regaining full-time employment. Workers in France had better social protection, and those still at work complained that wages did not rise while costs invariably increased, so they were also becoming poorer.

In order to be clear on this issue, which is closely related to most of the others in our table, let us review the fundamental causes. Standard of living has two main components, namely, disposable income and quality of services such as health, education, and so on. Higher disposable income depends on having employment and salary rises that require economic growth of more than 3% per annum, which was no longer being achieved.

Economic growth can come from consumer expenditure, exports, or investment, be it private or public. In the United Kingdom growth was due to consumer expenditure on the back of rising house prices; in the more prudent continental European countries, this (fortunately) did not happen. Exports were invariably declining as other countries produced their own goods. Private investment was low partly because of the high interest rates to keep down inflation; most of the investment that was made was directed at (often delocalized) facilities overseas. Therefore, there remained only one possible source: public investment, but in the most heavily indebted countries, this was restricted by the European Union (EU) debt criteria to a maximum 3% of gross domestic product.

This same factor made it impossible to improve quality of services—indeed governments sought to reduce expenditure there in order to have funds to invest elsewhere. (There were some other potential methods of getting out of this dilemma that will be brought out in the next chapter.)

Having dealt with budget constraints, we can now look at a similarly difficult situation in terms of balance of payments (B of P). While we saw that exports were declining, imports were increasing particularly from products made in China, other Asian countries, Turkey, and so on. Some of these products were manufactured in facilities previously delocalized from Europe; many services were similarly delocalized to India (in English) or North African countries (in French). The imports of energy and various raw materials that were at very high prices in early 2008 were added to this imbalance. Overall, therefore, B of P deficits were rapidly rising everywhere. Ways to tackle this problem, which seems to have been put into the background at present, will be discussed in the next chapter. The auxiliary issues regarding employment, like effects of demographic trends (aging population), lack of candidates for many types of available jobs, and the possible contribution of immigration in these areas, will also be covered.

Issues for International Action

The following issues go across national frontiers and can only be resolved by cooperation between countries:

- Political instability, terrorism, crime, corruption
- Ecology: pollution, waste, water, famine, sustainable development
- Globalization and poverty
- Rising prices of oil, raw materials, basic food items
- Financial instability

The first three issues have been under discussion for several years, and it is not an objective of this book to go into great detail about them. Most of the comments will therefore relate to the others.

It is paradoxical that *conflict situations* have become worse rather than better after the end of communism in the Soviet Union. The Mafia, Islamic terrorists, and others have been able to operate more freely after the end of the cold war.

Corruption seems to flourish equally well (or even better) under capitalism as it did under the more repressive communism. It is still very prevalent in the former Soviet bloc countries, even those now hoping to join the EU.

The *ecology* issue is finally being taken seriously, perhaps too much so as there is a lack of coherence in the measures being considered. An example of such incoherence was a campaign by a French airport to attract low-cost airlines to maintain its growth rate in the face of approaching competition from the far less polluting high-speed train being brought to their region (with considerable infrastructure investment). Otherwise, the reductions in emission gases planned in Europe will hardly be significant compared to those emanating from the millions of new cars to be launched in India, China, and other developing nations. Among the government-sponsored measures, allowances to scrap older cars (done mostly to help the automobile industry) will also slightly help reduce pollution, but many of these cars were still in good running order and could have served the less well-off citizens. Similarly, the proposed carbon tax is a laudable initiative but its imposition during a recession and rising unemployment, when people are just recovering from the recent oil price peaks, is a highly insensitive decision. Overall, if it is really true that the same reduced pollution effect can be achieved by halting the deforestation in the Amazon delta, would it not make sense to help the Brazilians achieve this objective?

The related issue of *sustainable development* is obviously anathema to certain manufacturers who want to maximize their production in the "throw-away" society. A personal example of this was the advice given to throw away a 5-year-old refrigerator in very good condition just because it was not economical to replace the failed compressor.

Regarding *globalization*, its defenders have always stated that it has reduced world *poverty*. To some extent, particularly in Southeast Asia, this is largely true, but, on an overall basis, if it has slightly improved the situation for all, it has done much more for the wealthy countries and the very rich people in every country.

It is somewhat disconcerting to have poor African countries seek more aid from North America and Europe, whose citizens are becoming less well-off, when some other countries like the Gulf states are spending fortunes on palaces and skyscrapers in their region.

Spring 2008 was, of course, the period of massive increases in the *prices of oil and many other raw materials*. To a large extent, these were driven by speculators on the future markets assisted by forecasts of certain analysts (which the media did a disservice to publish), who suggested that oil prices could reach a level of $200 per barrel. While enriching themselves, these unscrupulous people tried to make us believe that it was the high growth rates in China and the decreasing reserves that were responsible. As if Chinese growth of 10% rather than the previous 7% could really cause oil prices to double in such a short time!

I made this point in communications to several influential politicians and even suggested a number of possible methods to counter these practices, but no one seemed to have the will to initiate such measures preferring at most to provide some financial assistance to the very poor oil-heated households. We had to wait for the financial crisis later in 2008, and the ensuing specter of recession, to save us from this particular problem. If no one was willing to challenge the oil speculators, it is hardly surprising that problems from other noncontrolled areas would eventually come to the surface. The bank failures and subprime crisis of 2008 was, however, far more violent than anyone could have expected. Again, only a few remarks will be made here on a topic that has by now been extensively discussed everywhere.

The following issues need to be considered when analyzing the sub-prime mortgage crisis of 2008:

- The original idea of building homes for the less wealthy Americans surely has moral merit; in many countries like France, they are struggling to build enough lodgings for thousands of people who are on waiting lists. If the new owners were subsequently unable to meet their payments, why not allow them (with government help) to rent, paying what they can afford? And, anyway, houses and apartments are a useful nonwasting asset, unlike many others.
- Many European banks were involved in this fiasco. Is it because the expected returns were so much better than elsewhere? If so, does that not normally imply a much greater risk?
- The main response of the powerful nations to the crisis was to provide funds for the banks to be able to resume their lending activities. However, the banks will first want to repair their balance sheets and then probably look for better returns than to lend to firms or individuals during a recession.

For quicker assistance to the latter, I made suggestions to bypass the banks and have them merely serve as agencies to distribute government loans. Moreover, such loans could even largely come from savers like the French Government's Livret A scheme. (In September 2009 this idea was taken up by the small German town of Quickborn with a municipal loan provided by its citizens.)

During a 50-session crisis conference in Rennes, France, in March 2009—attended by 18,000 people—several of the speakers and a large part of the audience felt that there were too many deficiencies in the present financial systems for them to be corrected by the measures now being planned. A frequently expressed view was that there were too many financial institutions with too many people wanting to make too much money; the whole system needs to be reinvented from the top to bottom. But, of course, there are powerful interests and lobbies against such a change, which no politician would therefore dare to initiate.

Effects and Responses for Companies

The 2008 financial crisis continuing into 2009 is, of course, having a devastating effect on most companies. This will be examined under several different headings.

Activities

Under *operational and current activities*, most companies are simply trying to survive, for example, by shedding labor and reducing fixed overheads in order to lower their break-even point. In many cases they are going downmarket so as to serve the increasing number of customers who now find themselves short of money.

Regarding *strategic and future activities*, they are trying to identify what the after-crisis environment will look like. One thing that already looks likely is that there will be a more equitable balance of the rewards among the different stakeholders than has occurred in the past. A one-third split of profits between shareholders, workers, and investment has found favor among many political and business leaders in France. More firms are likely to go private and even organize themselves on alternative management models like cooperatives of the Mondragon type (Fagor, Brandt) in Spain's Basque country. These can be more flexible at times of crisis as there are no dividends to pay to shareholders, investment can be halted, and workers are more likely to agree to salary cuts in order to maintain their jobs.

Regarding *domestic versus international investment*, the situation is likely to favor the former to take advantage of government aids in key areas like energy savings, as there are few countries unaffected by the crisis that might offer better opportunities.

An example of a firm that has already taken onboard what they see as the requirements of the future is the French travel agency Voyageurs du Monde, which now has sales of €250 million. They share one-third of profits with their staff, who own 10% of the company. As a contribution to a clean environment, they donate €5 to €10 per flight taken to a Brazilian reforestation foundation.

Business Sectors and Functions

Within essential sectors like restaurants, it is already possible to see the downward movement toward fast food outlets and sandwich bars as opposed to sit-down establishments. In nonessential sectors, it is more difficult to forecast who will do better (like sports goods outlets) and who will do worse (like travel firms). Within the company itself, the two functions most affected are, of course, marketing because of lower demand and finance because of the great shortage of liquid funds. The human resource management department is having to bear the brunt of the crisis in dealing with redundancy and unhappy workers.

Processes and Skills

Readers will certainly have observed my enthusiasm for planning; however, the year 2009 is probably the first (and maybe only) year in which *planning*, at least of the continuous nature, will have to be put aside. The external environment is so uncertain that companies cannot really think far ahead until there is more clarity and stability in this area. What is of paramount need at this time is maximum flexibility to take advantage of existing opportunities or of identifying any new ones. Conceptual skills, such as innovation and new approaches, are therefore highly valued.

The *organization* must also be more flexible with people ready to take up different tasks or those from others who have been made redundant.

Leadership should try to be more humane regarding staff reductions and find ways of motivating those who remain. Ethical and exemplary behavior in sharing problems with the staff will be greatly appreciated.

Control, particularly of expenditure and cash flow, assumes a dominant importance in the battle for short-term survival.

Conclusions

The series of crises reviewed here highlight the need for companies to constantly adapt to sudden upsets in their environment. But the major issues being faced since 2008 are putting a much greater onus on national governments and international cooperation to create a more closely regulated and more stable climate in which firms can develop their business. However, because there are usually several ways of tackling each issue, it will be difficult to obtain agreement among so many nations as to how to proceed. Even if growth resumes in 2010, individual citizens must somehow survive, as forecasts suggest that it could be 2012 before the standard of living for most recovers to mid-2008 levels.

CHAPTER 8

How to Better Manage Our (World) Affairs

Introduction

The aim of this chapter is to examine some of the current problems in the national or international environment to see whether certain management techniques developed in previous chapters for business or companies can be applied to help resolve them. This kind of approach could be valid since companies have long been used to living and adapting to a changing and competitive environment much more so than have nations. The text will discuss *systems, policies, and management processes* taking examples from the geographical areas of western countries, the EU, or the developing world.

Political Systems

As soon as one brings up the issue of the inefficiency of our political systems, one might be told, "Maybe so, but they are part of our democratic process and far better than anything else"—by that implying a dictatorship without any opposition. For such people, democracy consists of an election every 4 years and the winning party (with often only 52% of votes) dominating proceedings until the next election. There is then usually a swing the other way and a reversal of many of the policies which that had previously been put in place. "Three steps forward and two steps back"—no wonder so little progress is made! As for the opposition, they tend to oppose almost everything, including even certain wise measures, as it is not in their interest (for the next election), that the ruling party has too many successes. This confrontational set up is rooted in the face-to-face layout of the "mother of parliaments," which is the British House of Commons.

This situation is made worse by the continuing use of the labels of the Left (Socialist) and the Right (liberal or capitalist), which were maybe appropriate before and after World War II but are no longer now. Attempts to launch center parties somewhere in between the two have not been very successful as voters cannot clearly see where these parties stand (partly socialist, partly capitalist?).

Yet there is a third alternative, and it can be found within the motto of the French republic—that is, "fraternité" or solidarity. It can be represented as in Figure 8.1 by the third (top) corner of a triangle rather than as something on the line in between the left corner (egalité or equality) and the right corner (liberté or liberty), with their respective connotations of communism and capitalism. During the present difficult times, a fraternité approach would almost certainly evoke strong popular support

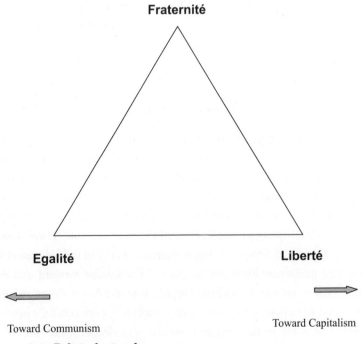

Fraternité

Egalité   **Liberté**

Toward Communism   Toward Capitalism

Figure 8.1. Political triangle.

in many countries, except those where "individualism" has become much stronger than "collectivism."

If this suggestion could be a useful step forward, there is perhaps an even better solution—albeit much more difficult to put into practice. This would involve the abolishment of political parties altogether. Candidates would be elected to parliament as independents and once there would choose the best available ministerial team to do their best for the country rather than any party. Instead of constant opposition, there would be a continuous debate as to how best to proceed; alternatives could be selected on the basis of a majority vote and this would include any eventual replacement of ministers or even the prime minister. There would be no need for street demonstrations against such a government as it would really be "the people's government" that is in power.

What links are there between these options and the business and company analyses in the previous chapters? There are indeed close parallels in that the existing "winner takes all" party system is analogous to the current "most profits for the shareholders" situation. The suggested fraternité or solidarity party concept would be equivalent to a more equitable profit distribution among *all* the stakeholders as is now being widely advocated. And the nonpolitical party idea resembles cooperative and similar "management alter" concepts (now taught in certain business school programs), where directors, workers, and shareholders are the same people all pulling in the same direction and equally sharing the rewards.

Leadership Process: Nations

From the wide range of topics covered in the leadership discussions of chapters 2 and 3, we can select a few that have a major influence on everyday problems at this time. The first concerns the characteristics of the leader that, we saw, fall under two main types. The more ostentatious, leadership-oriented type, pushing for change and fast results, would be type A. The more demure, management-oriented type, handling complexity and efficiency, would be type B. The former are often elected at a time of crisis for which they can be quite effective (e.g., Margaret Thatcher). They tend to have strong partisan supporters and equally strong opponents. Some of their policies are not well thought out and eventually lead to problems (e.g., excessive privatization). Nearly all want to stay in power too long and are finally rejected at the polls.

The latter, type B (e.g., Helmut Schmidt), perform well, face much less popular opposition but run the risk of becoming too passive or of being replaced too soon by newly arriving type As. Closely related to the above is the question of power balance in each individual national system. Whereas companies more and more appreciate the dual roles of a chairman and a chief executive with a supervisory board, many countries put all the power and representation in the hands of one person. If this "president" is also the leader of one political party, how can we expect the people who voted for other parties to become allegiant to him or her (e.g., George W. Bush)? In the worst cases, such a system favors serious corruption and dictatorships that are very hard to remove (e.g., many African countries and the former Soviet republics).

Western European nations with monarchs (e.g., Spain) or senior statesman presidents (preferably not past politicians, e.g., Vaclav Havel of former Czechoslovakia) can advise elected prime ministers against extreme measures and thus help maintain the stability of the country in the face of the ever more frequent street demonstrations. Obviously it is extremely hard to change to such a system—it is just a great pity that in exporting democracy to newly liberated nations, we did not make this part of the "package."

Control Process: National Economies

The blatant lack of controls that led up to the subprime crisis has been widely discussed everywhere, and some pertinent comments on it have already been made in chapter 7. This short section covers the much less dramatic, but more frequent, control of inflation and growth that was the major preoccupation in early 2008. At that time Western European growth was hit by high inflation largely resulting from the rapid price rises of oil and other raw materials. It was thus not possible to reduce interest rates even to maintain growth that had already been at a low level due to various factors including the high euro to dollar exchange rate. This predicament should have confirmed to everyone what is known to most engineering students, namely, that one cannot control several variables with only one single lever (interest rates)—especially as the level of interest rates also affects the exchange rate.

Other types of controls should have also been brought into action to suppress inflation (e.g., price controls) or to increase growth rate (e.g., extra government spending). Unfortunately, this last solution is itself subject to a quite different control, namely, the European Union (EU) limit of deficits not exceeding 3% of gross domestic product—which many countries were already exceeding. If this limit has now been virtually abandoned in the face of the subprime crisis, could it not have been slightly eased then? Clearly we need to study the different possible control options and establish quantitative predictions (e.g., what change in growth rate for 1% change in interest rates) so that suitable responses are available for the next time such situations occur.

Planning Process: National Economies

It is almost impossible to bring up the subject of planning in the national context without being told that it is something that demonstrated its failure in the communist epoch of the Soviet Union. Yet, as we have seen in the early chapters, planning is practiced by most companies and certainly those that have the best performance records. Communism can be condemned for its suppression of personal freedom and failure to supply enough products in the shops, but it did provide the minimum essentials (lodging, bus travel, healthcare, etc.) for the population at affordable cost. Its replacement by rampant capitalism in several countries has created a small number of very rich and a large number of poor. The Chinese, on the other hand, have shown that a communist system with a partly planned and controlled economy can produce significantly better results—even than those achievable in a noncommunist state.

In western countries, the liberal or capitalist model gives companies and entrepreneurs complete freedom of action to create and grow their firms as they may desire. Hoping that this will automatically create the best results is like hoping that a pack of cards thrown up into the air will fall down in the right order. Indeed, it is amazing that the system has achieved what it actually has! However, its limitations have become evident during recent years. Private sector firms have been overproducing not only cars but also many other household goods while there are substantial shortfalls and a declining level of quality in more essential areas like housing and education. These latter areas are, of course, largely funded by governments who have lacked money to invest in them. Even worse, governments have been burdened with paying unemployment benefits when the private sector firms go bankrupt or make workers redundant.

There is clearly a need to adjust this balance in favor of providing the more essential items for the population, and this could be done through planning incentives, appropriate taxation policies, and others. Some reflection on this subject suggested new methods of raising government revenue other than by taxing companies or workers, both of whom already find themselves in difficult situations.

The principle was to identify areas of large flows of money or of less essential products or services on which a small percentage tax could be levied without much harm to the participants. What happens to national lotteries could thus be extended to company acquisitions, football transfers, luxury products like large-screen televisions, and mobile phone text messages. A quick calculation for France showed that a tiny two-cent tax on the latter would bring the state no less than €800 million.

A further extension would be to combat tax evasion by emigrating individuals (e.g., in entertainment) by taxing their payments at source—that is, on the organization in the country where they are earned. Another sizeable contribution could come from a more significant property tax on luxury homes and secondary residences, which are relatively unproductive assets.

Overall, therefore, the whole taxation system requires a thorough overhaul so that it helps to "drive" the economy in the optimum direction. Thus, applied taxation rates could vary by sector so that true wealth-creating institutions and workers in essential areas (law enforcement, health, etc.) only have to pay very little, while less necessary and exotic products and services (e.g., yachts, art auctions), typically advertised in glossy magazine supplements, are taxed more severely. Would this not be a very worthwhile concept for the European Commission to examine?

In addition, the present recession is emphasizing something that has been evident for a few years but not much talked about. That is, *how are we here in the West going to earn our living? What products and services are our workers going to produce that can be sold overseas to pay for the imports of raw materials and other goods that we buy?*

A decade ago the answer was "advanced technology," but this is now equally available to the Koreans, Chinese, and others. Lately, we have been selling many aircraft to such countries, but they are now setting up their own production lines (often with our help). The only major product categories that seem to remain are nuclear power stations and advanced armaments. (Although, South Korea just beat France, the largest user country, to win the Abu Dhabi nuclear power station contract.) A similar situation is arriving in services with Indian software companies, airlines from the Gulf states, and others. Western nations will therefore have to rely more and more on the sector of tourism where there could be a huge influx of newly rich Asian visitors (there are already more wealthy Chinese than Europeans).

These issues must be urgently addressed within the context of some overall blueprint for many reasons apart from the obvious balance of payment deficit. One of the main reasons concerns the future of the students now in higher education who are becoming very concerned about their eventual jobs. With the overseas transfer of much manufacturing and many services, they may find themselves limited to local service jobs of the estate agent, optician, or fast food outlet variety, which have started to dominate our high streets (McDonalds will be the biggest French recruiter in 2010). Unfortunately, most of these do not require graduate-level qualifications and are not paid at rates that they might have expected. Overeducated people are now becoming quite common; this is a frustration for them and a waste of money for the state or others who have paid for their education.

Setting arbitrary targets (e.g., "50% of young people should attend university") without having first assessed what jobs will need to be performed is a naëve and wasteful approach. More places and lower fees should be made available for the training of professions that the country badly needs. At the other end of the age spectrum is the growing problem of the people over the age of 50 whom companies try to push out but whom governments want to stay on—now even beyond age 65—to accumulate sufficient funds for their retirement. Thus, young people cannot find jobs (20% are out of work in some Western nations), seniors are retired early, and those in employment are facing increasing stress. What a recipe for misery and social unrest! Any future deliberation on educational institutions and employment has to take into account these overall national activity questions. Moreover, nothing can be treated in isolation as every aspect is related to others. A typical current example concerns the deleterious effects of redundancy and unemployment on worker sickness (health service investment) and crime (prison enlargement).

How do we prepare the recommended blueprint? By using some of the planning techniques described in the earlier chapters. Specifically, for the national entity by identifying the most urgent needs like housing, nursing, and directing training and infrastructure investment into those areas. Internationally, by critically analyzing the competitive position of different sectors and encouraging human and financial resources to be moved there rather than being dispersed too widely or into areas where success is unlikely (further discussion in chapter 9).

Organizing Process: European Union

Several years ago when the EEC and the European free-trade area (EFTA) were merged to form the EU, I drafted an article questioning whether the EU project had been sufficiently well thought out from an organizational point of view. The original EU vision of incorporating Germany with France and some others had quietly been transformed into creating a much bigger grouping to rival the United States on which it was partly being modeled. This was quite inappropriate as the 50 American states were very similar in nearly all aspects and their citizens were proud to be known as Americans and nothing else. Quite a different situation from the Europeans who not only spoke different languages but also were more attached to their own particular country (or even region) rather than to an eventual EU.

From a management point of view one could therefore envisage a high degree of complexity, problems of communication, coordination, representation, and difficulties in getting widespread agreement on various issues. Ingenious solutions were found for some of these, like the triple roles of commission, parliament, and rotating presidency, but this, coupled with parallel governments in the individual countries, presented a highly complex equation compared to major trade competitors like the United States, Japan, and later China and India. The requirement for unanimous decisions on items like the level of value added tax posed a further restriction on flexibility and potential for rapid action. Finally, there was little foresight as to the eventual size and membership limits.

The installation of a common currency is certainly a unifying factor, but the advantage of quick price comparisons between various countries is of little relevance to most people who shop in their own and, without sufficient safeguards, saw large increases in prices of many everyday goods. Since that time, ordinary people wonder exactly what benefit they, as individuals, get from the system and whether these benefits justify the costs of the operation.

While obviously appreciating the removal of travel, study, and work restrictions, there is the genuine criticism that the *European Commission* spends too much time on harmonizing trivial details and ensuring maximum competition among member state firms rather than defending them against external competition and threats from outside the EU. If central and eastern European countries joined the EU, it was because they hoped they would get long-term preferential treatment regarding exports, inward investment, and so on, compared to outsiders like China.

The EU Parliament does carry out some serious legislative work (which is little known to the man in the street), but it is of a more medium-term and thus less urgent nature, which then has to be agreed and implemented by the national parliaments. It is, therefore, not surprising that citizens, already unhappy with the speed of reaction of their own parliaments, don't give it much attention—as reflected in the very low turnout at the recent European elections. *The rotating presidency* is an equitable formula but too variable in terms of personalities and of their inherent priorities. An obvious alternative is that of a full-time president during a period of at least 1 year, but there seems to be a shortage of people of sufficient stature for such a post, especially if it is to be agreed upon by at least a majority of the 27 members. (See the postscript at the end of this chapter for more information.)

Overall, therefore, the scope for organizational change within the EU institutions is now rather limited. The one aspect where there is still some flexibility is the eventual number of members. While the small Balkan countries will need to be integrated as they cannot really exist on their own, the more distant states like Georgia and big countries like Turkey and Ukraine can only hope for some form of associate membership if the organization is not to become completely unwieldy.

International Aid Policies

This short section is dedicated to the subject of international aid and, particularly, to ensuring that aid given to poor countries reaches the population for whom it is destined. Donors have been extremely naïve in this regard so that most of the aid is in fact creamed off by the leaders in the recipient countries. There is a need, therefore, for a much tougher stance in this respect for which some suggestions are given in the following list:

- As much as possible of the aid should be given in the form of donor-supervised projects rather than money. Typical projects could be constructing and equipping a new hospital or garbage incinerator, both of which are sadly lacking in such countries.
- Tax havens and banks should be compelled to identify large sums deposited with them by corrupt leaders from poor countries. Such money, as well as luxury properties bought by these leaders in democratic nations, should be sold, and its proceeds put into an appropriate aid fund.
- During natural disasters such as the recent flooding in Myanmar, medical agencies like the Red Cross should be provided with helicopters based on UN-leased vessels to deliver aid directly to the populations concerned without having to wait for local government permission. Any attack on these helicopters could be justifiably punishable by air strikes.
- Modest immigration quotas to the EU should be fixed for cooperating countries but only on the basis of a temporary stay (say, 1 year) in order to enable these immigrants to learn a trade and earn some money. Otherwise, it is patently unfair that a few should be admitted on a permanent basis while so many others are never given a chance.
- Wider use should be made of the example of Villa El Salvador in Peru where thousands of displaced persons, given some land and displaying great solidarity, succeeded in establishing a new town environment for themselves.

A New Sense of Values (ANSOV)

In the face of the multitude of problems and bad news constantly arriving in the international environment (the H1N1 flu being the latest at the time of writing), it is comforting to see some signs of attitudes changing in positive directions.

The response to pollution and carbon dioxide emissions by cars has been truly dramatic to the extent that small and hybrid cars have ousted 4×4 and high-powered sports cars from the covers of many automobile magazines. A similar sense of responsibility is becoming evident with regards to the voluntary trimming of payments received by top company directors. How far can such a movement progress?

The ANSOV concept I suggest envisages a continuing shift from individualism to collectivism and to a world that admires individuals not for their accumulated wealth but for the contribution they have made to others in society. Out go magazine articles of the "hundred richest people" to be replaced by something like "the man or woman of the week." Excessive and ostentatious wealth would be looked down upon—if not actually despised, much as it has been to some extent in Scandinavia for several years.

Business people, for example, would be admired for the new (useful) firms that they launched or the number of new workers that they hired rather than for how much money they earned by justifiable, legal (or dubious!) methods. (A good example at time of writing is the Italian small firm owner who shared part of a large lottery prize with his crisis-affected employees.) Such a system would bring a human being's innate desire regarding professional objectives and those of personnel fulfillment closer together—and for many with their religious faith. It should therefore obtain the full support of churches of all denominations.

To opponents having something to lose, the ANSOV concept would soon be classed as a version of communism—which it patently is not. To cynics, the concept would be seen as completely unrealistic in practice, but, if it certainly is closer to idealism than pragmatism, it is less so than many other noble visions like those of eliminating world poverty or ensuring a global system of justice. A major question that remains is how, besides public recognition, these valiant people could be rewarded. Certainly not by money prizes as this would destroy the whole idea. One possibility would be to enable them to become philanthropists distributing the financial value of any awarded prizes toward particular causes that they wanted to support.

Conclusions

The diverse examples selected have illustrated how many of the management techniques originally developed for business can also be used to help resolve problems in nonbusiness areas. In addition, such analyses have helped to identify possible new approaches that normally emanate from the application of the conceptual skill of "innovation." In a January 2002 article in the *Financial Times*, John Lloyd asked, "What can be the next big idea to civilize the dominance of liberal democracy and capitalism?"[1] Since that time we have been encountering more and more frequent problems in this regard. Hopefully, the three suggestions made here regarding changes to political and values systems will be a useful contribution to this debate.

Postscript on the European Union Organization

As noted in the previous section of this chapter, in mid-November 2009, a candidate, namely the Belgian Prime Minister Herman Van Rompuy, was chosen as EU president. The selection process (by the heads of government of the 27 member states) seems to have been chiefly based on having a person acceptable to all the nations and to the main political parties in the EU Parliament and who would not "upstage" the strong character of the leaders of the larger countries. Thus the role for this person was designed as the "president of the council of (prime) ministers," which is like that of a representative and committee chairman rather than a true leader. (The six monthly rotating national presidencies would continue.) A rather quiet person, the new president is certainly a very competent man and his skills of tact and securing consensus will help smooth out the frequent conflicts within the community. However, once again (as had previously been discussed in this text), the EU has shown that it

---

[1] "Wanted-the next big idea "1/12/2002

is more concerned with harmonization and smoothing out internal problems within the community rather than fighting for its external interests in the world. For the latter, a stronger personality of greater stature would be required to face up to the "heavyweight" leaders on the world scene such as Barack Obama, Hu Jintao of China, Vladimir Poutine of Russia, and Benyamin Netanyou of Israel.

CHAPTER 9

Conclusions, Review of the Past, Changes for the Future

Conclusions on Previous Chapters

After providing a rapid summary of good ways to manage, the text identified and discussed numerous examples of management failings. Most of these were attributed to individual staff or managers but many to the companies or various organizations—national or international—in which they worked. The analysis was generally based on one of the five managerial processes or the relevant skills associated with it (e.g., leadership process and communication skills).

Some of the examples were relatively trivial but others were very significant in terms of eventual consequences, be they financial or human.

As a rough guide, one can say that *planning* errors can lead to missed opportunities; *organizing* errors can lead to nonoptimum performance; *leadership* errors often cause important failures; and *control* errors can, in the worst case, cause big disasters.

A supplementary benefit of the process or skills approach used in this text is that these are aspects of management that do not change much with time; many others do and problems have arisen by not appreciating this fact—as will be discussed in the following sections.

Management Practice: Past

On the company side, management practice had a steady evolution over 25 years until 1985, when John Nisbet made the startling predictions that there will be radical changes toward the information society, services, empowerment, the learning organization, and so on, which actually came about in the 1990s. Numerous authors assumed the situation would continue in this new vein well into the future, even risking such titles as "management in the 21st century." However, as growth rates declined and financial greed became common, cooperation between directors and workers (or even directors and managers) turned to friction and animosity. Low cost by any means, especially delocalization, started to become more important than staff cooperation, or even than the much advocated "attitude toward customers" factor (as in the case of one or two European low-cost airlines).

On the government economic policy side, there was an unwise prolongation of practices reckoned to be appropriate at that given time—but even then with only mixed results. Notable among these was that of *privatization* or *deregulation* being justified as an attempt to improve the quality and to lower prices for the consumer but in fact was driven by the desire of governments to reap some funds while avoiding the need to make necessary investments. Of course, this policy did produce a number of successful results, but in too many cases it caused the consumer much confusion without reducing prices and sometimes even affected safety through lower expenditure on maintenance by the new owners. One of the most ridiculous examples was the privatization of the efficient French telephone enquiry service that attracted a dozen candidates from which the consumer then had a hard time selecting the best—as most in fact charged significantly higher prices than had existed before under France Telecom. It would have been far better in many cases to create mixed state and private enterprises as occurred in several other instances of nationalized firms in that country. Other examples of the bad consequences of privatization relate to new private owners creaming off profits without making sufficient investment: this brought about a collapse of the New Zealand railway system that had to be subsequently renationalized.

Another questionable policy was that of maintaining the development of sectors where there was already *considerable overcapacity*—particularly automotive and its hundreds of suppliers. A similar example is that of airlines flying with many empty seats across the Atlantic and yet somehow surviving despite recurrent losses. Of course, these sectors generated much employment, but relatively little effort was made to develop others like ecological or renovation of infrastructure. It only required a severe drop in demand, as arrived after the recent financial crisis, to see the unfortunate consequences of such practices.

On the international dimension, there existed the supposed panacea of *continually increasing trade*. In the beginning, this concept, sensible in theory, brought large benefits to consumers in terms of greater availability of goods at lower prices. However, as it progressed, it led to closures of factories in the West and large increases in the volume of freight sent by road, sea, and air. An absurd example of such activity was the export of French timber logs to China in order to be transformed into parquet flooring that was then reimported back to be sold at 10% to 15% cheaper than could have been the case otherwise. If the ensuing energy waste, pollution, and nonemployment effects were taken into account, would this kind of practice still be valid?

Management: Modifications for the Future

The financial and economic crisis of 2008 was a real watershed, probably equal in significance to Nisbet's predictions. It will modify so many aspects of doing business that it is too hazardous to make anything but outline predictions. (In retrospect, many of these modifications should already have been initiated even if the crisis had never arisen.) Governments and international organizations will probably take over the leading role in industrial development from companies partly because of the critical nature of certain factors such as climate, partly because they will be the main available sources of finance, and partly because of the need for establishing controls that are still not in place (on July 1, 2009, a lone trader moved up the price of oil $7 per barrel overnight).

Numerous *privatizations* have been reversed through the *nationalization* of several banks and subsequently certain firms in other sectors (e.g., train operators in northeast England). Hopefully there will be encouragement to produce (and not overproduce) really useful products and services as *excessive competition and overcapacity* are wasteful on resources. Many services involving simple selling-on of goods create very little added value and should perhaps be taxed at higher rates. (Possibly the most stupid example is the UK practice of buying and selling special letter combinations of car number plates.) With regards to *trade*, it would be wise to mainly import only what you cannot make. (This limited protectionism is already coming into evidence in China.)

It is necessary to start measuring benefits as a *total package*—including items such as pollution and energy use—rather than just financial returns. Novel products such as electric cars need to be exploited judiciously, bearing in mind that they are a response to combat local not total pollution, and that reaping their full benefits will require modifying sociological factors as well as the technological, which has not yet been undertaken.

Governments are finally tackling *the excessive pay issue*—at least for bonuses being paid to bank traders. There really needs to be some relationship of the amount one gets paid to the amount of effort he or she provides: a large company president may well deserve $1 million for a year's work, which cannot be compared to a trader's few minutes of brilliance on a computer screen. Athletes work hard, but the salaries for the best are now at around $50,000 per day! Most of this money comes from company sponsors who obviously think they get a better deal from a $10 million sponsorship than from taking on 100 extra workers to expand their business. Have we thought out the eventual consequences of such behavior?

Many elements of management practice developed for business organizations could well be applied to governments, as some already have been to individuals (e.g., that of planning one's life in terms of career, marriage, finances, etc.). Thus, nations could adopt the company planning process in terms of mission, goals, strategy, actions, and by various measures such as special incentives and tax credits, seek to align the interests of the individual with those of the nation.

An *overall mission* should include the quality of life factor rather than just growth (which brings with it associated problems as well as benefits). Thus, the notions of gross national product and gross domestic product might well be shared with the *concept of individual happiness or well-being*, which is attracting increasing interest following several recent publications (e.g., New Economics Foundation) and a reflection solicited by the French government from two Nobel Prize winners. The example of Bhutan, a poor country that has already started to measure happiness ratings, is a laudable example.

Each country needs to carry out a *national competitiveness evaluation*. This consists of two key elements, namely, assets and transformations to be directed outward or inward. Most western nations now have fewer assets and a reducing volume of transformations to be sent outward. They will therefore have to obtain most of their future income from the inward movement of people (e.g., tourism) and products (perhaps via duties on imports from countries with whom they have a very negative trade balance), since the large spending power of their populations is their greatest remaining advantage—which has somehow to be better exploited.

Like the ecology issues, the rather somber picture painted here has not appeared suddenly and is not due to the financial crisis (which will, however, make it more difficult to resolve). It could be traced back to around the start of the 21st century with the growing world impact of China. Politicians were not sufficiently concerned about this because some observers said it would be a transient phenomenon like the dominance of Japan in the 1990s. But there are hundreds of millions of poor Chinese in the countryside willing to replace those who may seek too high a level of wages in the towns, so the China example could last for 50 years rather than 10.

Considerable modifications in approach in all spheres will therefore be needed and these should provide scope for research in universities and business schools to compensate for the fact that much existing course material—especially relating to topics such as international business and finance will no longer be valid.

Postscript

Is it possible in a few paragraphs to explain the lack of progress in so many of the worldwide problems described in the last chapters? Most of them, like air pollution, youth unemployment, and decaying infrastructure are not new but have been getting worse for several years. That so little has been done to alleviate them, despite having plenty of available labor, is to a large extent due to a shortage of associated capital.

Most governments had already built up large amounts of national debt to burden future generations and the now huge volumes of private capital (the 300 richest bank accounts in Switzerland represent $300 billion) do not flow to these key problem areas. Rather, they search for the higher returns to be found in luxury products like villas on tropical islands, in commodity speculation, and other such investments even though these may carry higher risks that can lead to failure (e.g., Dubai World estates in November 2009).

More money must therefore be made available to governments for dealing with these critical problems on which our tolerable existence depends; some suggestions (avoiding the conventional solutions of cutting essential services or raising income taxes) have been made in chapter 8 of this book. Even then, with the continuously increasing world population and their demands for at least basic items like food, water, medical care, and shelter (nearly 3 million people lack decent housing in an "advanced" country like France), the battle may not be won unless there is some miraculous breakthrough somewhere; thermonuclear power is perhaps the only such thing that can be envisaged at this moment.

When we bring up these kinds of dramatic issues, the in-company case studies given within this book pale into insignificance. Except perhaps that, if managers applied good management to handling the smaller issues, they might have become more adept at dealing with the big ones?

APPENDIX A

Case Study

The Rio to Paris Plane Crash

This case discusses management errors that could have contributed to this tragedy

Introduction

A decision was made to write this case study since it is relevant to many of the topics discussed in this book and even brings in some new ones. It also has a personal significance to the author, in as much as a friend died in the crash and another luckily survived by taking an earlier flight.

Recapitulation of Facts

Flight AF447 was the Air France A330 Airbus evening flight from Rio to Paris with 228 passengers and crew. It disappeared over the Atlantic between the Brazilian and Senegalese air traffic control (ATC) stations on June 1 2009 without having given any voice distress signals except for some subsequently transcribed printout data indicating problems with air speed measurement and computer control systems. A widespread sea search during the following month recovered several pieces of the aircraft and some bodies. The "black box" flight data recorders were not found in the ocean, which is very deep in that part of the world.

Constituting Elements

Certain elements need to be evaluated in this type of accident, namely, the weather, ATC, the passengers, the aircraft, the crew, the airline, the control agencies, and others who organize world aviation.

Weather conditions on the route were certainly forecast to be very bad, but it was left to the pilots to go around the heavy thunderstorms that often occur in that part of the equator. Unfortunately, these two engine planes do not have the flexibility of taking much wider diversions, being required to minimize the distance flown between control stations in case of one engine failure. However, the manufacturers stress that their aircraft are capable to withstand these conditions as has been proved "hundreds of times in the past." But climatic conditions are becoming more violent, perhaps on one of these occasions, the weather will be too severe?

ATC could do nothing for them as there is no radar coverage that far out and the controllers had no weather data on their screens to warn the crew.

The passengers also appear not to be relevant since there was no sign of an explosion due to terrorism on the recovered aircraft parts (except for the remote possibility of someone disabling the pilots to ditch the plane). The aircraft was modern and generally well maintained although there had recently been a history of problems with certain makes of pitot tubes (bought in from external suppliers), which measure air speed on these planes. In one or two cases, like an A340 flight from Tokyo to Paris several months before, the crew had a hellishly difficult time to bring the plane under control. Were pilots on such long range routes familiar with this case, and were they trained on how best to handle a similar problem were it to arise?

The flight crew was certainly very experienced. This was one of the first questions asked after the accident, but, ironically, it is a double-edged factor. If we need a superexperienced pilot to land on the Hudson River, could there be a tendency for such a pilot to be overconfident regarding his or her abilities to tackle extreme weather conditions—which a less experienced pilot would avoid by rerouting, delaying the flight, or even making a stopover at the last available airport before the ocean?

A relevant incident happened to a relative recently driven to the airport but whose flight was delayed 15 minutes because the pilot preferred to circle overhead rather than land during a violent thunderstorm. After landing, he even refueled to make sure he would have enough gasoline to deal with possible similar conditions at his return destination. Recalling the 2005 accident of a plane during a scheduled landing in a violent storm at

Toronto airport (where passengers had to scramble out in a muddy field as the plane caught fire), I hope this pilot is complimented rather than criticized by his (low cost!) airline for slightly upsetting their timing schedule.

The *airline* policies and procedures are thus very significant to these situations. To what extent are scheduled upsets and higher costs acceptable to ensure 100% safety? The fact that the airline needed a threat by the staff union to boycott the planes until the pitot tubes were changed is a scandal on the behavior of its top management.

The European *control agency*, in this case AESA (European agency for aviation safety), must also take a large share of responsibility. They exist precisely for the purpose of safeguarding the public interest in the face of inadequate practices by airlines, manufacturers, or others. Several weeks after the crash they finally made a ruling on the mandatory replacement of the pitot tubes by all airlines flying these planes. If they did not feel it necessary to have gone that far beforehand, they should at least have imposed some restrictions such as forbidding these type of aircraft from flying on the most dangerous weather routes and certainly forbidding the aircraft to fly out of range of ATC radar.

The *organization of world air transport* also requires certain improvements to assist in the clarification of eventual accidents such as the following, for example:

- The most important black box flight recorders are of little use in cross-ocean flights. Huge amounts of effort and money are spent in searching for them, mostly without success. Surely there must be a way of designing them so as to separate from the plane to be able to float for usage on such routes? Alternatively, money should be spent on greater usage of already existing equipment that continuously sends aircraft data information via satellite.
- At a time when ordinary car drivers have sophisticated phones and global positioning system (GPS) units, why can't the pilot of a plane flying outside air traffic control zones be able *immediately* to switch to an emergency radio channel so as to at least describe his problem? Even if a crash may not eventually be avoided, at least coastguard planes could be scrambled quickly to identify its position and thus help subsequent recovery efforts.

Conclusions

As in most accidents there is likely to be more than one main cause—in this case, probably the very rough weather and the pitot tubes. However, the various parties have exhibited management deficiencies—particularly regarding leadership, risk taking, and control, which need to be addressed.

The aircraft manufacturer must better control the quality of his subcontractors and to clearly define the weather conditions that would put the plane in danger. The pilots should avoid overconfidence in their abilities and take the safest action even if under pressure from their employers. The airlines must correct any items that have previously caused bad incidents more rapidly, retraining pilots in this regard and really putting safety before schedules and cost. They are not like other service sector firms where risk taking at worst cause only financial and job losses. The controlling organizations must ensure that all these actions are carried out or impose total or partial flight restrictions before any serious accident occurs.

Regarding the last discussed items of flight recorders and radio, everyone should understand that aircraft crash deaths are not to be compared to (the many more) cases arising from car accidents. The aircraft passenger has had no personal responsibility in the accident and no means of having being able to avoid it. For many crashes in midocean, no one learns of the exact circumstances as there are no survivors, and, possibly worst of all, the bodies are not recovered so that relatives cannot attend a funeral and pay their last respects to the victims.

Postscript

A report analyzing the crash was published in early October by two pilots, one retired and the other the president of the pilots union. They confirm and further develop the items covered in this case study and also bring out some further points such as the disturbing detail that pilots are given charts on meteorological conditions 24 hours in advance even though these can, of course, radically change at the time they actually fly.

They also contrast the prudent and rapid reaction made by the small Air Caraëbes airline after two of their aircraft suffered similar problems several months before. The fact that most AF pilots were not shown all reports on these events, never mind trained how to handle such situations, is a major flaw in the company's communication and operations.

Just prior to this report (on September 23), the airline described the various corrective measures that it had taken since the crash and its intent to carry out an independent external security review "to reduce the possibility of such an event happening again." This is not a very dignified phrase to use in these circumstances and highlights the sad fact that loss of life is taken too lightly in the company.

It is incredible that such philosophies exist in previously state-owned firms (also Renault, France Telecom), in which the French government still has a significant shareholding (around 15%) and presumably a representative on the board of directors who has clearly failed in one of his key duties.

However, there now exists a strong prosafety emphasis within the airline's operations as demonstrated by the fact that, on December 2, a similar plane (even with reliable pitot tubes), made a detour to avoid strong turbulence in the same zone where AF447 had crashed. It is only highly regrettable that so many lives were sacrificed to arrive at this situation.

APPENDIX B

Application to the Management of Soccer Matches

This section analyzes shortcomings that could be overcome to improve the game.

Introduction

A soccer match is an event like many others that can be effectively organized even by a group of students according to the five management processes—as frequently done in the author's management course assignments (see chapter 2). However, what is attempted here is something original and quite different, namely, management during the match itself as it takes place on the field. The analysis will nevertheless be based on the same elements that have been used throughout this book such as objectives, skills, roles, and processes.

Objectives of the Event

The two main objectives of a crowd-attracting event are normally customer satisfaction and financial receipts sufficient at least to cover all the costs. However, in a competitive environment, winning has become so important that, in most cases, the quality of the spectacle takes second place. One of the strange observations in this sport is how (mostly not very wealthy) people will pay substantial sums every 2 weeks to watch many boring matches—presumably, the experience of being with other fans in the stadium is what matters. In some cases, like the 1996 UEFA European Football Championship, the many boring matches were aggravated by lots of bad decisions and players sent off the field for foul play.

Actors: Roles, Skills, and Behavior

The three categories of actors on the field are, of course, the players of the two teams, the two coaches, the referees and linesmen, and, in the background, the football authorities who set the rules and impose sanctions where necessary. What roles, skills, and behavior are pertinent for these actors to ensure a successful event?

Coaches are often former players, though not usually of the highest fame since those kinds of players cannot easily make the necessary transition from performance of self to that of developing others. He is knowledgeable in these required skills, although he sometimes has a technical director or an assistant to reinforce the technical aspects (especially for goalkeepers). His role is to select and prepare the players before the match and to analyze the team performance afterward. However, his role during a match is somewhat contentious: Is he supposed to continually direct the manner in which the team is playing? If so, then the players are like pawns in a chess match; why don't the players wear a radio earpiece so they can precisely obey his instructions? Under such circumstances one then wonders what the role of the team captain is supposed to be (see the "Leading" section).

Players are largely selected on the basis of their technical playing skills, their physical state, their mental approach, and their interpersonal fit with the other players. However, each player has his particular best role, be it in attack, defense, midfield, or goal, and these cannot readily be altered.

On analyzing the technical skills of the individual players, one is surprised at the deficiencies even in those playing in the premier divisions and earning thousands per week. The following are just a few examples:

- There is a widespread inability to pass the ball and to shoot at the goal with either foot—something that many an average college player has trained himself to do.
- Large numbers of passes and shots at the goal are completely off target, which is ridiculous bearing in mind the size of the goal. Contrast this with ice hockey players who do far better even when moving at much greater speed and having a very small goal as a target.

- There are very few innovations: 90% of the action is largely stereotyped (although this is partly due to coaches imposing minimum risk tactics). Again, this could be contrasted with certain other sports such as American football where much of the action is less predictable.

The soccer referee is a high-profile figure who can either stay in the background of a smoothly flowing game or completely upset the rhythm and outcome of the match. The latter type exhibits behavior that we have already discussed in the chapter sections on bad bosses. Thus, the man may quickly wish to establish his authority by sanctioning with a yellow card even a minor disagreement. This means that one more even modest contravention committed by the same player subsequent to this sanction gets him a red card, and he is then sent off the field. If this type of procedure is to work, there should perhaps be more yellow cards or a sending off for only a limited time—again, as in some other sports. A complete sending off should be reserved for the most serious offenses only.

The other big weakness of referees is in decision making, especially at the time of a possible foul around the penalty area. Again, the football authorities have not helped him (e.g., by using video as in tennis), and his decision, usually taken from a distance in a very short time, is frequently wrong. As most matches these days involve very few goals, awarding a penalty shot and a likely goal will often decide the result of the match. Referees thus become very unpopular with spectators—and could become corruption targets for the various betting organizations.

The football authorities as we have seen don't do much to help the work of a referee, but they do invariably uphold his decisions (even if wrong) to the great annoyance of clubs and supporters. In fact, they seem to be an excellent example of a "resistance to any change" body as discussed in chapter 2.

Some years ago our consulting firm sent in a detailed proposal to award the three points for a win only to teams having won by more than one goal; otherwise, the win would only count as two points (as was the case a long time ago). Such a system would encourage teams to search for more goals to the benefit of crowd entertainment, and, with a larger goal difference, victory would be more clear-cut as it is in almost every other sport; any bad referee decision would also be less consequential. Even though there seems to be no disadvantages to such a system, no reply to this proposal was ever received. Presumably, any idea that is not "home grown" will not be considered by them. But then, if the fans continue to come to matches and the television or betting pools continue to pay for rights, they may feel that it is not necessary to make any changes.

Management Processes

Planning

Most of a team's success seems to emanate from occasional individual skills or by chance actions during the play. Only a few situations, especially for free kicks, seem to be planned, but this could be done for many others in order to catch the opponents off guard and perhaps secure that vital first goal.

Organizing

By an imposed organizational pattern like 4-4-2 (the numbers of defenders, midfielders, and attackers), the positions of the players are rigorously adhered to. This reduces the risks from opposition attacks but at the same time kills off much innovation, thus making the game less exciting—and losing opportunities to score goals. A balance needs to be found between organizational rigor and flexibility for different periods of the match.

Leading

Leading is mostly done from the touchline by gestures from the coach. The captain seems to mainly have a role of motivation, setting a good example to the other players, and dealing on their behalf with the referee. Is this indeed the optimum working method, or should it be modifiable according to the captain's skills?

Control

Control needs more attention. Far too often the ball is given away to the opposition by goalkeepers and passes directed to marked players. All of these items need to be worked through in training and improved, together with the other weaknesses like shooting on target previously mentioned under technical skills.

Conclusion

This initial attempt at applying management practice to real-time events has hopefully achieved two results: Firstly, it should have shown business analysts a methodology that can be used for similar situations elsewhere and in the future. Secondly, it should enable the various parties involved in soccer matches to reevaluate and improve some of their existing practices. There is a current tendency to transfer some of the sporting strengths to business, so equally in the other direction, sporting events should be able to benefit from successful business practice.

Postscript

On November 18, 2009, 2 months after this text was written, occurred an event that fully demonstrates the relevance of the points made in this chapter. In a match of the highest importance to decide on the one remaining vacancy in the 2010 South African World Cup, a controversy erupted that reached prime-minister level. The cause was a deciding goal for France against the Irish Republic after a player had pushed the ball with his hand to the scorer of the goal. This fault was presumably not seen by the referee, who allowed the goal to stand. Subsequent video replays and even the player's own admission confirmed this fault. What is responsible for such a situation occurring? Initially, two items that had previously been discussed might be the following:

- The *environment* where so few goals are scored that one goal can be so critical.

- The *decision-making process* where the football authorities obstinately refuse video or any similar technological assistance to help the referees.

But here, in addition, the *lack of initiative of the referee* himself: in this particular case, he could have responded to the Irish protests by a direct question to the French player, who would not want to risk a serious suspension by telling a lie. Also, this could be thought of in terms of the *ethics* of the player himself, although he probably acted on impulse in the heat of the situation and considered decision making to be left to the referee. He admitted and regretted his action afterward and even supported calls for the match to be replayed. If he could only have brought himself to immediately announce his fault on the field to the referee, then it would have greatly raised his personal stature and set a wonderful example for all those wanting to clean up a sport where the level of sportsmanship is well below that of many others (e.g., rugby, golf).

APPENDIX C

Detailed Contents

Planning

- Mission, goals, strategies, plans, actions
- Continuous plans (every year for 3–5 years)
- Strategic plans (periodic, "where do we want to be?")
- One-off plans, e.g., small firm start-up or launching major event
- New projects (why, where, who)
- Timetable (+ PERT chart?)
- Problem solving (groups, sequence/methods, alternatives/constraints)
- Decision making (free discussion, consensus, importance, speed)

Organizational Structure

- Centralization vs. devolution (depends on culture, degree of control, staff availability)
- Departmentalization by function, product, place, hybrid, matrix (depends on importance of rapid response vs. duplication, cost)

Organizational Style

- Bureaucratic/mechanistic (hierarchy) or organic (flat) (depends on nature of environment, age/size, plus for manufacturing: on technology process (continuous/batch)
- Services: on whether routine or nonroutine

Organizational Change

- Transformation based on "hard" issues, e.g., reengineering and "soft" issues, e.g., empowerement, resistance

Staffing

- Selecting, hiring, training, evaluating, promoting, parting, future planning

Leading/Directing

- Leader behavior: carrot and stick, democratic/autocratic (depends on leader needs, nature of followers, situation)
- Leader orientation: human/broad/flexible or task/detailed/rigid (largely depends on leader's personal character and background)
- Motivation and respect (individuals/groups, methods, absence)
- Communication (internal/external, up/down, formal/informal)
- Delegation (what, to whom, how, benefits, resistance)
- Management development (skills, coaching, psychology)
- Managers vs. leaders (complexity/efficiency vs. change/effectiveness)

Control

- Four financial statements (profit/loss, balance sheet, cash flow, break even)
- Budgets, financial ratios (liquidity, leverage, profitability)
- Operations activity (stocks, capacity)
- Projects (within time-frame, budget, quality norms)
- People (performance evaluation)
- External control (auditors, nonexec administrators, regulators)

Figure 10.1. Management processes summary chart.

Index

Note: The italicized *f* following page numbers refers to figures.